GLENCOE

Inclusion in the Consumer Classroom

Margo Vreeburg Izzo, Ph.D.
Director of Special Education and Transition Services
Ohio State University
Columbus, Ohio

Sarah K. Guider
Executive Director
Starboard Education
Columbus, Ohio

New York, New York Columbus, Ohio Chicago, Illinois Woodland Hills, California

Contributor

Kendra Naef
Family and Consumer Sciences Instructor
Kimberly High School
Kimberly, Wisconsin

Technical Reviewers

Ina J. Kirstein, M.A.
Consultant, Assistive Technology
Oakland Schools
Waterford, Michigan

Marsha Markle, M.A., M.A., Ed.S.
Personal Coach, former School Psychologist
Coronado Unified School District
Coronado, California

Sandra Harris, M.A.
Learning Disabilities Teacher-Consultant
Cherry Hill Board of Education
Cherry Hill, New Jersey

Bethany Broadwell, B.A.
Freelance Journalist, Specializing in Issues
Pertaining to People with Disabilities
West Bloomfield, Michigan

Glencoe offers a special thank you to the following Ohio teachers who contributed their classroom experiences with inclusion during the development of this supplement—Julie Hartsel, Linda Taylor Knight, Sandra S. Kemerer, and Shelly Williams.

Brand Name Disclaimer

Publisher does not necessarily recommend or endorse any particular company or brand name product that may be discussed or pictured in this booklet. Brand name products are used because they are readily available, likely to be known to the reader, and their use may aid in the understanding of the text. Publisher recognizes other brand name or generic products may be substituted and work as well or better than those featured in the text.

Internet Disclaimer

Any Internet listings given are a source of extended information related to our booklet. We have made every effort to recommend sites that are informative and accurate. However, these sites are not under the control of Glencoe/McGraw-Hill, and therefore Glencoe/McGraw-Hill makes no representation concerning the content of these sites. We strongly encourage teachers to preview Internet sites before students use them. Many sites contain links to other sites, and following such links may eventually lead to exposure to inappropriate material. Internet sites are sometimes "under construction" and may not always be available. Sites may also move or have been discontinued completely by the time you or your students attempt to access them.

Art Credit
Gorman & Associates Inc.

The McGraw-Hill Companies

Send all inquiries to:
Glencoe/McGraw-Hill
21600 Oxnard St., Ste. 500
Woodland Hills, CA 91367

ISBN: 978-0-07-876789-0
MHID: 0-07-876789-X

Printed in the United States of America

1 2 3 4 5 6 7 8 9 024 10 09 08 07

Contents

Activity Plan Contents

INTRODUCING INCLUSION IN THE FACS CLASSROOM

Why offer a teaching resource for working with students with special needs? Since its introduction, the Individuals with Disabilities Education Act (IDEA) has been changing classrooms across the United States. With inclusion at the foundation of this legislation, IDEA focuses on protecting the rights of students with disabilities and their families. Students with disabilities, just like *all* students, have a right to the best possible education that accommodates their needs. Along with the daily demands of teaching, the inclusion of students with disabilities in the classroom creates additional challenges for teachers. Through this resource, we at *Glencoe/McGraw-Hill* hope to offer you some helpful strategies for meeting the varied requirements of your students with special needs.

As a Family and Consumer Sciences (FACS) educator, you teach the essential skills that are required to live independently. Skills including career development, money management, food preparation, household management, parenting, and family relations are critical for students to possess to live on their own. All students need these skills, including students with disabilities and students who are at-risk of failing due to emotional, social, or economic issues. The phrase "students with special needs" is used to describe these students who require special supports and accommodations to access, learn, and apply the content you are teaching.

This booklet offers you a wealth of resources for teaching students with special needs. The various sections offer strategies for integrating students with special needs into your classroom using a variety of teaching strategies, supports, and accommodations.

Key Terms for Inclusion in the FACS Classroom

Accommodation—A change in how an academic requirement (e.g., assignment, assessment) is presented or how the student demonstrates competency, which may include changes in the presentation format, response format, setting, timing, or scheduling. This term generally refers to changes that do not significantly alter the requirement. It results from a student need; it is not intended to give the student an unfair advantage.

Assistive Technology—A broad range of devices designed to increase, maintain, or improve the functional capabilities of a student with a disability. Assistive technology may include equipment or product systems. It allows people with disabilities the same access to information and production as their peers.

Attention Deficit Hyperactivity Disorder (ADHD)—A neurobiological disorder that interferes with a person's ability to sustain attention or focus on a task and to control impulsive behavior. If the inability to sustain or focus attention occurs without hyperactivity, the condition is referred to as *Attention Deficit Disorder (ADD)*.

Auditory Aids—Equipment or software items designed or used to compensate for a person's total inability to hear or limited ability to hear. The auditory aid(s) used depends upon usable residual hearing and preference. Auditory aids allow students with hearing disabilities the same access to information and production as their peers.

Auxiliary Aids—Equipment or services designed to compensate for functional limitations related to disability and that allow equal access to course content. Examples include—but are not limited to—services, such as interpreters or note takers; adaptive technologies, such as voice input or voice output computer software; alternative media, such as braille texts or video captioning; or adapted work stations, such as a lab table lowered for wheelchairs with modified equipment for participation in lab experiments.

Cognitive Impairment—A generic term that refers to a heterogeneous group of disorders characterized by significant difficulties in the acquisition and use of listening, speaking, reading, writing, reasoning, or mathematical abilities, or of social skills. These disorders are presumed to be due to central nervous system dysfunction. A cognitive disability may occur concomitantly with other disabling conditions (e.g., sensory impairment, mental retardation, and social and emotional disturbance), with socio-environmental influences (e.g., cultural differences, insufficient or inappropriate instruction, psychogenic factors), and especially with Attention Deficit Disorder (ADD), all of which may cause learning problems.

Deaf/Hard-of-Hearing—Conditions characterized by total inability to hear or by limited ability to hear. Individuals who are deaf or hard-of-hearing vary considerably and, depending upon usable residual hearing and preference, may use different types of auxiliary aids and accommodations. Some speak; others use very little or no oral communication.

Disability—As defined by the Americans with Disabilities Act (ADA), a disability is "(A) a physical or mental impairment that substantially limits one or more major life activities of an individual; (B) a record of such an impairment; or (C) being regarded as having such an impairment."

Dyslexia—Neurobiological in origin, dyslexia is a specific learning disability that is characterized by difficulties with accurate and/or fluent word recognition and by poor spelling and decoding abilities. Other consequences may include problems in reading comprehension and reduced reading experience that can impede growth of vocabulary and background knowledge.

Lab Adaptations or Assistants—These accommodations consist of using specialized equipment (such as assistive/adaptive technology) and/or the assistance of a lab attendant to help with the completion of tasks in a laboratory setting.

Learning Disabilities—Permanent disorders that interfere with integrating, acquiring, and/or demonstrating verbal or nonverbal abilities and skills. Processing or memory deficits are frequently associated with learning disabilities. Individuals may have difficulty with reading, spelling, written expression, mathematics, problem solving, listening, and oral expression. The disorders are often inconsistent and each individual has his/her unique set of characteristics.

Medical Disabilities—Individuals with medical disabilities may exhibit several functional limitations. Some types of conditions that may fall under this category include, but are not limited to, diabetes, seizure disorder, juvenile chronic fatigue syndrome, multiple chemical sensitivity, or muscular dystrophy.

Mobility Impairment—A disability that limits an individual's ability to move; walk without the aid of a wheelchair, walker, or some type of assistive device; or walk long distances due to situations, such as limited energy or chronic pain.

Psychiatric Disabilities—Disabilities that involve some type of diagnosed emotional and/or mental illness. Individuals who have these disabilities may exhibit inappropriate types of behaviors or feelings under normal circumstances, have a pervasive mood of unhappiness or depression, develop uncontrollable fears associated with personal or school problems, and a multitude of other characteristics. These characteristics are generally beyond the individual's control, but may be helped with treatment.

Seizure Disorders—These disorders include epilepsy or other types of recurrent seizures.

Seizures—A seizure is an electrical misfiring in the brain. Seizures can range in severity from being virtually unnoticed to episodes with convulsions or loss of consciousness. Seizures usually come on very suddenly and can vary in duration. A seizure may occur only once or it may occur repeatedly.

Text-to-Speech—The automatic conversion of written text words from a computer document (e.g., word processor document, Web page) into audible speech spoken either by a synthetic (computer-generated) or digitized (recorded) human voice.

Visual Aids—Equipment or software items designed or used to compensate for a person's total lack of sight or limited sight. The visual aid(s) used by a student depends upon usable residual vision and preference. Visual aids allow students with visual disabilities the same access to information and production as their peers.

Visual Impairment—A disability that involves either a total lack of sight or limited sight. People who are visually impaired vary considerably. For example, some have no vision; others are able to see large forms; and still others can see print if it is magnified.

SECTION 1: FAMILY AND CONSUMER SCIENCES (FACS) SKILLS FOR ALL LEARNERS

Most high school students dream of the day when they will move into their own places, declare their independence, and make all of their own decisions. The information and skills learned within the Family and Consumer Sciences (FACS) classroom greatly support this dream. Yet, how do these courses and the skills taught within them benefit all learners, especially students with special needs?

Benefits of the Inclusive FACS Classroom

Inclusive classrooms tend to offer a "win/win" situation for both the typical learner and the student with special needs. Including all learners in the classroom is the best way for everyone to understand how diversity enhances the learning process while providing a balanced education for all. Here are some additional ways that students benefit from inclusion:

- ◆ A welcoming, inclusive environment promotes learning about others, teaching respect, and recognizing that everyone has strengths, gifts, and challenges.
- ◆ All students tend to show an increase in acquiring new skills and greater compassion for their peers as they work through the learning process.
- ◆ Students with disabilities have increased interaction with their peers which promotes the development of communication and social skills.
- ◆ Self-esteem increases as all students embrace the diversity of their classmates which in turn increases cooperation.
- ◆ Typical learners demonstrate a greater acceptance of individual differences among their peers and an increased ability to develop friendships.

Tapping Student Strengths

Every student learns differently. Each student has strengths and weaknesses. When a student has a special learning need, it is up to the teacher to provide what is necessary to assist that student in becoming a successful learner.

Many students have strengths that may not be obvious within traditional classes, such as math, English, or science. However, within the FACS classroom, students with disabilities can be successful for several reasons.

- ◆ First, FACS classes teach daily living skills. For example, students have an opportunity to learn about nutrition, how to prepare food, budget their resources, or explore the challenge of raising a family.
- ◆ Secondly, FACS classes often use a hands-on approach. Students may talk about how to cook, see the equipment, supplies, and ingredients, and then get to actually cook a meal. In this case, the teacher taps into the visual, auditory, and kinesthetic learning styles.

Recent studies indicate teacher expectations change outcomes far more than educators have ever realized. Robert Rosenthal, Professor of Psychology at the University of California–Riverside, says teacher expectations can become a self-fulfilling prophecy. When teachers expect better school performance from all of their students, it tends to happen. Therefore, you have a powerful opportunity to create change.

As you prepare your lesson plans, think about ways to develop activities in which everyone can demonstrate their skills and competencies in meaningful ways. The passages and sections that follow offer a wealth of information to help provide all of your students with the best possible education.

Who Are Students with Special Needs?

A recent Roper poll shows more than 20 percent of all students may encounter significant school-related difficulties. Approximately one-half of the students with difficulties complete psychological or medical assessments to help identify their disabilities. Today, over five million students with disabilities have been identified in public schools throughout the United States.

Students with disabilities have diverse cultural backgrounds that cut across racial, ethnic, and socio-economic categories. Most students share a deep desire to experience success and feel good about the schoolwork they produce. No student needs to fail; however, some students need special education services to be successful. *Section 3, Special Education Policies and Practices*, provides an overview of special education services.

A federal law called the Individuals with Disabilities Education Act (IDEA) impacts all schools across the United States. This federal legislation has protected the rights of students with disabilities and their families since 1975. It specifies that to receive federal funds, every school system must provide a free and appropriate public education for every student regardless of any disabling condition.

IDEA mandates that the U.S. Department of Education report the number of students who receive special education services. Therefore, every local school district must turn in an unduplicated count of students served to its state department, who then submits the data to the U.S. Department of Education. See Figure 1-1.

It is important to have a common understanding of the definition of the term disability. **Disability** refers to any student who:

- Has a physical or mental disability that substantially limits one or more major life activities, such as talking, walking, or self care.
- Has a record of disability, such as a student who no longer has a disease but is still trying to educationally catch up with his or her classmates.
- Requires special education and related services to realize his or her full potential.

Figure 1-1

Number of Students Ages 6 Through 21 Who Were Served by IDEA in 2000-2001

Disability	Number of Students	Percent of Total
Specific Learning Disabilities	2,887,217	49.99%
Speech or Language Impairments	1,093,808	18.94%
Mental Retardation	612,978	10.61%
Emotional Disturbance	473,663	8.21%
Other Health Impairments	291,850	5.05%
Multiple Disabilities	122,559	2.12%
Autism	78,749	1.36%
Orthopedic Impairments	73,057	1.26%
Hearing Impairments	70,767	1.23%
Developmental Delay	28,935	0.50%
Visual Impairments	25,975	0.45%
Traumatic Brain Injury (TBI)	14,844	0.26%
Deaf—Blindness	1,320	0.02%
All Disabilities	**5,775,722**	**100%**

Source—U.S. Department of Education, (2003), *Twenty-fourth Annual Report to Congress on the Implementation of Individuals with Disabilities Education Act* (p. II-20)

The U.S. Department of Education publishes an annual report to Congress, which details the number of students receiving special education services. The latest statistics show a change in the types of students served. Nearly 50 percent of the students identified under IDEA fall into the category of Specific Learning Disabilities. (See Figure 1-1 on page 9.) Regardless of the categories used, the number of identified students receiving special education support continues to grow.

The term "at-risk" describes a student who does not have a special need or disability, but is considered at risk of failing school and not graduating due to emotional, social, or economic issues. At-risk students may not qualify for special education services. *Section 2, Meeting the Needs of All Learners,* has many teaching strategies that will benefit at-risk students.

In the passages that follow, definitions, case studies, common teaching strategies, and accommodations are provided to help you meet the special needs of learners in your classroom. In this booklet, students with disabilities are categorized into the following broad areas:

- Students with invisible disabilities, such as specific learning disabilities or emotional disturbances.
- Students with sensory, orthopedic, and mobility disabilities, such as those who are blind, deaf, or use wheelchairs, crutches, or other orthopedic devices.
- Students who have cognitive impairments.
- Students with autistic spectrum disorder.

Students with disabilities require specialized education for a variety of reasons. Some may learn differently than their regular classroom peers, some may be physically impaired and need adaptive equipment, or others often require specially designed instruction to benefit from their education. This instruction is individualized and is updated annually in a student's *Individualized Education Program (IEP)*. See *Section 3* for more information on the IEPs.

Nutrition & Wellness Skills

In FACS classes, students learn about nutrition and food preparation and explore healthful life choices. Learning about household equipment, kitchen utensils, appliances, and how to maintain fitness broadens the student's knowledge base.

Think about your classroom organization. Can the student who uses a wheelchair navigate your classroom safely? What cooking skills can be safely and successfully demonstrated in your room? Do you have a classroom with lowered work surfaces to accommodate a wheelchair? Is the hand-held equipment sturdy? Do the handles have a good grip? In this case study, see how Mrs. Knight made accommodations for Alex, a student with multiple disabilities.

Case Study

Learning to Cook

Alex used his wheelchair to move himself closer to the countertop. It was his turn to cook the pancakes. He watched his partner measure the liquid ingredients into the big plastic bowl. When this was completed, Alex took the bowl. His grip was steady as his hands grasped a specially designed spoon. Alex used his other arm to hold onto the bowl. The specially designed bowl had a rubber grip to keep the bowl from slipping. Using the folding technique taught in class, Alex worked hard to blend the mixture as his partner slowly added the dry ingredients. Alex knew he needed his partner's help to pour the mixture into the hot skillet. After pouring the first couple of pancakes, Alex and his partner used the spatula to lift each one to test for doneness. By placing their hands on the handle together, they turned each pancake over successfully!

Following Up By working together, each student was able to leverage his or her strengths to cook as a team. The buddy system works.

How do you establish a lesson plan that includes everyone in the classroom? Some students have skills while others struggle. One suggestion is to look for ways that students can demonstrate competency while leveraging their strengths. Think about a student struggling with writing. Allowing students to develop posters or presentations as alternatives to a written paper accommodates those students who struggle with written expression. Some teachers allow students to create mobiles to display their knowledge, take verbal exams, use study guides during quizzes and tests, or use demonstrations to show their competency.

Consumer Skills

Many students are concerned with how they will handle the pressures of daily life once they move out on their own. When students understand the impact of money, they begin to realize that they will soon be depending upon their own skills to manage money. Some just want to learn how to make wise purchases with the money that they have. The knowledge gained in FACS classes impacts many students on a daily basis for the rest of their lives.

All teachers should attempt to reinforce a student's ability to read and solve simple, everyday math problems. Imagine the student who has never before managed money. In the following case study, Denise, who has a learning disability, teams up with a friend to complete a goal and participate in a school project. Because of her disability, she may always need someone to help her with some of her daily skills; however, in the case study, see how Denise leveraged her strengths to learn a new skill.

Case Study

Learning About Budgets

Denise and her classmate, Janie, decided to get an apartment together. They decided to use this as their Consumer Education class project. Denise and Janie will need to plan a budget, determine where to live, and select furniture. Denise had a part-time job and knew how much money she had to contribute to the monthly living expenses. She and Janie used the traditional budget categories discussed in class to help determine how much money they could spend in various categories. They decided that some basic furniture would be a large, one-time expense for which to plan.

Using the newspapers and magazines provided by their teacher, Denise and Janie researched the furniture choices and costs. They created a portfolio of the choices and selected their favorite colors. Denise used a calculator with Janie's help to determine how much money they needed to save to buy all the furnishings at once. Next, she and Janie reviewed the apartment ads for possible places to live. When they had narrowed the list down to the top five choices, Denise and Janie made plans to visit each one with the assistance of their teacher. With the flyers from the apartments, furniture choices, and planned expenses, Denise and Janie are organized and ready to make their move after graduation. They discussed their final plans with their teacher and organized a presentation for class.

Following Up Notice how Denise learned how to plan for her own future. She used tools and supports to make it happen; yet, made her own decisions.

Students need to practice living within a budget. For those who have never handled money, newspaper and Internet ads can be helpful as students learn to practice their comparison-shopping skills.

Parenting & Child Development Skills

Many students think about marriage and becoming a parent. Students often think raising a child is not very difficult because their exposure to children is often through babysitting at times when children are happy and ready to play. Reality hits home in this class when students become aware of the self-sacrifice necessary to raise a child. Students discover the sacrifices every parent makes to see that the child is fed, clothed, and cared for on a daily basis. They begin to understand that having a child in the house is a lot of work and expense.

The lessons learned by each student will vary because of his or her own family experiences and ability to comprehend parenting techniques. One strategy to help students learn about the realities of parenting is to have them care for the computerized baby dolls that can be programmed to cry at different volume levels. Teachers can set the dolls to match every student's temperament and personality. This case study shows what a student with an emotional disability learned about the realities of parenting by using a computerized doll. Mrs. Martinez understood that Grace becomes easily frustrated and programmed the doll on the lowest setting to accommodate her needs.

CASE STUDY

Parenting with a Computerized Doll

Grace was excited! It was her turn to take the computerized baby home, and Grace was certain she would not have any trouble. All she had to do was feed, change, and play with the baby. Simple! Babies slept through the night, right? Okay, maybe this was going to be just a little hard. Grace was going to have to pay close attention to the baby. Mrs. Martinez knew Grace had trouble remembering information and became upset when under stress. Therefore, Mrs. Martinez customized the controls on the electronic baby specifically for Grace. By the end of 24 hours, Grace had learned how much care a baby really needed and how feedings or diaper changes often come at the most awkward times.

Following Up Grace learned an important lesson by being included in the project. Teacher accommodation of her special need allowed Grace to make important discoveries on her own. Her one-day experience of taking care of the baby doll was more valuable than a week's worth of lectures on parenting skills.

Family Relationship Skills

Most students realize that being at school is a great deal of hard work. Some enjoy it, while others do not. Each day many students watch their parents head off to work with similar feelings. Students may not realize that parents must balance the pressures of work with the equally demanding issues of raising a family. When it comes to understanding the delicate balance of work and family life, students often fail to see it is occasionally difficult to achieve an equitable balance between these demanding and sometimes contradictory responsibilities. See Figure 1-2.

Students need to understand their own physical, social, emotional, intellectual, and spiritual needs. However, they may not have thought about how their personal needs impact the family. They can probably see the results of their actions but may not understand how they contributed to the situation. If you add in the needs of the workplace, the student may become overwhelmed. Therefore, students need a safe place to practice or role-play learning these skills.

The following case study shows how Hank learned to accommodate all the family members' preferences when planning a family trip despite his disability. Students were introduced to the use of multiple sources from the school library for the project. In Hank's case, he needed to make use of some assistive technologies to tap into these library resources. Hank's teacher understood that if Hank could do a project that had relevance to his family, he would work harder on the project.

Figure 1-2 Students often find it challenging to learn the delicate balance between self, work, and family.

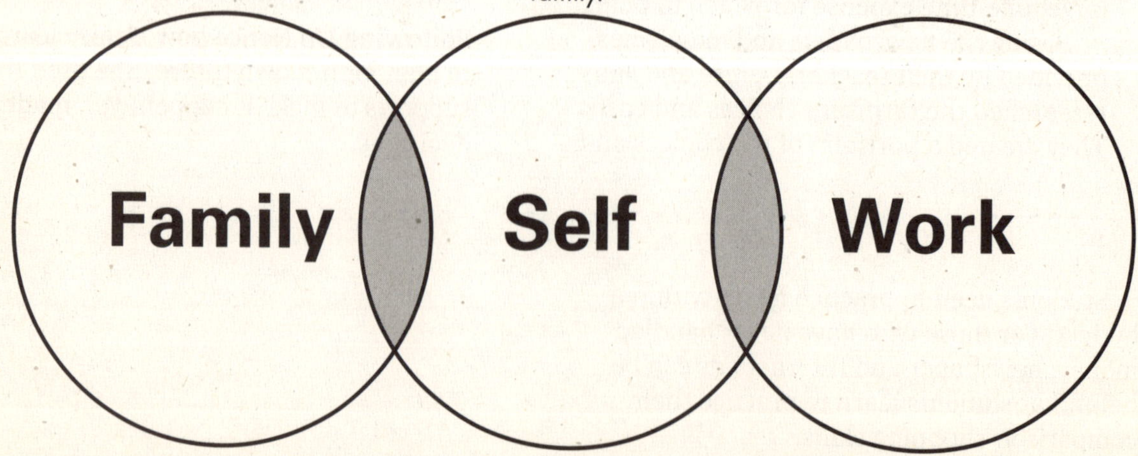

CASE STUDY

Planning the Family Vacation

Every year a different family member conducted vacation research and presented a plan to the rest of the family. It was Hank's turn to plan the yearly family vacation. He could even get class credit if he gave a presentation on the planning procedures he used. The twins wanted to play at the beach, his Mom wanted peace and quiet, and his Dad wanted to hit golf balls. Hank enjoyed sleeping in a tent and hiking with his older brother. Money was tight this year and the trip couldn't be expensive. Where was he ever going to find the perfect place? When could they go? How could he find a place that everyone would enjoy?

Using a voice synthesizer, Hank asked the family for work schedules. Then he grabbed some maps and settled down near the computer, and started working on his research. Wow, what a challenge! Using the problem-solving and budgeting skills he had learned in class, Hank soon narrowed the choices down to his top five and was ready to share with the rest of his family. With the use of assistive technologies and his notes, Hank would present the findings to his class. Hank was excited that he received class credit and helped out his family by planning the next family vacation.

Following Up As he learned to work with his family members and respect their ideas, Hank completed the class project. When teachers allow students to select assignments that are interesting to them, students will learn more. Hank had the incentive to spend hours on his project. He learned more than his teacher or parents ever imagined.

Personal Development Skills

Students need a safe place to work on improving skills that involve relationships with others. Within FACS courses, students discover the impact of their choices. Taking responsibility for your choices, learning to say no, and seeing the positive virtues in all people are only a portion of what students learn in this class.

Healthy Lifestyle Choices

Role-playing helps students understand sensitive topics that are difficult to discuss, such as making friends, dating, relationships, and saying "no." Developing simple scenarios that contain these complex subjects allows students the opportunity to openly discuss their attitudes. Scenarios are important because the complexities of these subjects are difficult for many students to understand. Sample scenarios are:

- You see a student in your math class that you would like to get to know better. How would you initiate a conversation?
- You finally have several conversations with the student and want to go to the movies. How do you ask this student out?
- You find yourself attracted to a student and have politely and appropriately tried to get to know him or her better. You keep getting the "brush off." What should you do?
- You are in a classroom working with several students. One of the students begins making sexually explicit remarks to you that make you uncomfortable. What should you do?

Sometimes a student needs to hear how others would react to a situation. Role-playing in class helps everyone understand that there is not always a perfect solution to a problem. Teachers should always encourage class participation, respect for others, and a willingness to include all students in the exercise.

Personal Grooming Choices

Students need to learn about personal grooming and what their image says about their self-confidence. Personal grooming can be a challenge for students with physical disabilities. The FACS teacher can use creative ways to teach these concepts, such as role-playing, videos, or class discussions. How can you create a safe learning environment that doesn't single out a particular student for ridicule? The following case study shows how one student changed himself to learn about others.

CASE STUDY

Observing Attitudes

Kevin decided to create an experiment based upon information he had just learned in class. Although he was well liked by his peers, he wanted to see if students treated him differently based upon his body language and choice of clothes. After all, he was the same person only he planned to look different for several days of class. Kevin talked with his teacher and learned the experiment would be acceptable as a class assignment. This was going to be fun! Kevin didn't tell anyone else about his project.

Kevin conducted his experiment over a period of three days. The first day he decided to wear colors that didn't match. The next day he buttoned his shirt haphazardly. The third he wore torn, dirty clothes and looked at the floor or out the window when speaking to his classmates.

After the experiment was over, Kevin pulled together all the information about people's reactions he had collected. During his presentation to the class, Kevin commented on how quickly his classmates began treating him differently during the experiment. Many of his classmates were surprised with the negative results of his study. Kevin even surprised himself with how much he learned about others and how much appearance mattered in some situations.

Following Up Kevin and his classmates learned a valuable lesson about how easy it is to judge others based on their appearances. Kevin found that his classmates talked about him behind his back and kept away from him because of his appearance. Even though they had accepted Kevin earlier in the semester, things changed when Kevin changed. Kevin and his classmates found out how unfair it is to treat others unkindly based on their appearances.

Career Development Skills

The need to work and make money is important to most students. Some students have had career goals in mind since childhood; others haven't a clue what they will do after completing their education. FACS classes provide a place to practice the skills needed to write résumés, dress for success, interview for jobs, ask questions, and dream of obtaining the perfect job. When you have students with disabilities in class, you need to make certain each student has a chance to practice these life skills. Whether students stay with one job their entire lives or change careers multiple times, the skills learned in your classroom will assist them with their choices. The next case study shows how Mike performed during a mock interview. Mr. Davis taped the class interviews and allowed students to grade themselves. These two simple strategies helped students take more risks.

CASE STUDY

Practicing Interviewing Skills

Mike was organized for the mock interview. He knew how to make polite small talk for a few minutes before the interviewer started with the tough questions. Mike quickly sat down in front of Mr. Davis and signaled the videographer to start the video camera. He answered each question politely and confidently and was sure he had not made any mistakes.

As the camera replayed the scene, Mike noticed some of his actions were distracting during the interview. Each time Mr. Davis asked a question, he tapped his foot repeatedly while he thought of a good answer. He also noticed that he repeatedly brushed his hair back in a distracting manner. Wow, what would the rest of the class see? Mike listened to his classmates constructively critique his performance, and he took notes on those things he wanted to change. Mike eagerly waited for the next interview ses-sion so he could practice his new skills. For Mike, it may take several practice sessions to eliminate some behaviors and build his self-confidence.

Following Up Sometimes being able to see yourself through the eye of the camera helps you understand how others see you. Mr. Davis allowed all students to see themselves as others see them when he recorded the interviews on tape.

Students need to explore different jobs in order to find one that fits their interests, personality, and skills. Job shadowing is an effective technique. Prior to job shadowing, students conduct research into career requirements, pay scale, and educational requirements. Teachers can support their students by asking parents in the community to volunteer as hosts for a job-shadowing day.

Core Academic Skills

Reading, writing, and math are key skills in everyday life. They are also required in most cases to obtain and maintain a job. All states require a minimum level of proficiency in reading, writing, math, science, and history/citizenship. Many states require students to pass high school exit exams in core academic areas in order to earn a high school diploma.

FACS teachers need to reinforce the importance of these core academic skills and strengthen student proficiency within their core curriculum. For example, when preparing food, stress the importance of comprehending the directions as students read recipes. If students don't understand a term or a direction, have them look up the term in a dictionary or glossary. Following recipe directions improves the look and taste of the food being prepared. In the same manner, following directions on proficiency tests improves test scores.

Reading in the FACS Classroom

Reading is one of the fundamental building blocks of student success in school. However, many students struggle to successfully decipher the words on a page. The U.S. Department of Education published estimates showing that 33 percent of the students entering ninth grade read two or more years below grade level. How can you accommodate the student who reads slowly with limited comprehension? You can use the following strategies and accommodations for helping all your students improve their reading skills. Find additional strategies and methods in *Sections 2, 4, 5, 6, 7,* and *8*.

Strategies for Teaching Reading

Teachers should reinforce reading skills in every classroom. Reading consists of three key skills: recognizing vocabulary words and being able to pronounce words correctly; understanding what the words mean when linked together in sentences and paragraphs; and fluency or being able to read and understand the written words with a consistent pace. Strategies for each of these reading skills are as follows.

Teach Vocabulary: Teach students the terms associated with your class by asking students to:

- Display words on bulletin boards, posters, or charts.
- Create flashcards with a key term on one side and the definition on the other side of each card.
- Practice using their flashcards through peer tutoring sessions.
- Monitor progress through charts and other assessment techniques, such as games, quizzes, and tests.

Improve Comprehension: Teach students to read with meaning by using these strategies:

- Provide an overview and the purpose of the reading assignments, giving students some of the questions they need to answer while reading. Or, discuss the questions in advance.
- Ask students to preview a recipe, chapter, or handout by reading only the headings, subheadings, bolded terms, and graphic titles.
- Divide reading assignments into small "chunks" and stop to discuss key points.
- Teach students to ask questions, take notes, and outline key points while reading and during discussions.
- Use concrete examples to illustrate the points made in a reading passage.
- Use peer tutoring or the buddy system to pair students to work together as they read and outline critical information.
- Provide overview handouts and guided notes (see sample of guided notes in *Section 2*).
- Recite, review, and demonstrate key points until students master the important content.

Improve Fluency: Improve the reading fluency of your students by incorporating the following strategies into your lesson plans.

- Provide advance notice for oral reading, encouraging students to practice independently or with a friend.
- Encourage students to relax—it's possible to read faster when a person is relaxed.
- Encourage students to move their eyes faster along the page. Have students make their eyes follow their fingers as they read quickly across the page.
- Focus on essential words, such as nouns and verbs, eliminating adjectives, adverbs, and conjunctions.

Reading Accommodations: Sometimes students' disabilities make reading fluently with comprehension impossible. For example, a student who is blind cannot read a print-based textbook. Use the following accommodations to help students work around reading challenges:

- Allow students to use assistive technology to listen to computerized materials or books on CD or tape.
- Allow students to use dictionaries and glossaries during all classroom activities and testing situations.
- Provide books on tape or CD in your classroom.
- Provide readers (other students or classroom aids) for students who cannot read the material.

By giving students opportunities to apply their reading skills in classes where they are motivated by the reading material, you will enhance your students' reading abilities.

Writing in the FACS Classroom

Writing can be a challenging skill because it requires the student to remember how to form letters, spell, organize thoughts, capitalize, punctuate, construct sentences or paragraphs, address a specific audience, and review the work for necessary corrections. Some students are not successful with all elements of good writing. Use the following strategies to help your students improve their writing skills.

Writing Strategies: Encourage students to use the following writing outline:

1. **Choose a topic.**
   - Write down what you know about the topic.
   - Write a thesis statement, or an idea that tells the purpose for the written paper. (Give students many examples of appropriate thesis statements.)
   - Identify your audience.
   - Ask questions that you need to research.
2. **Research your topic.**
   - Write down the questions that you want to answer in your paper.
   - Research the questions and write the answers on index cards.
   - Organize your cards to create an outline of your paper.
3. **Write the paper using a computer program with spell check and editing features.**
   - Write the introduction by stating the thesis.
   - Prepare the body paragraphs by writing the topic sentence and then the supporting facts.
   - Grab the attention of your audience by using vivid vocabulary and descriptions.
   - Write the conclusion by restating the thesis statement.
4. **Proofread and edit the paper.**
   - Teach students to use spell-check and editing features of word processors.
   - Teach self-regulation and assessment by setting deadlines for each of the steps listed above.

You can improve the writing fluency of your students by providing frequent opportunities to practice small writing assignments such as short essays on topics related to class. Provide frequent verbal and written feedback to students. Also, provide examples of both poor writing with corrections and quality writing samples.

Teachers can also help students improve their writing skills with the use of graphic organizers. These organizers can either be hand drawn or done on a computer. See Figure 1-3 on pages 17 and 18.

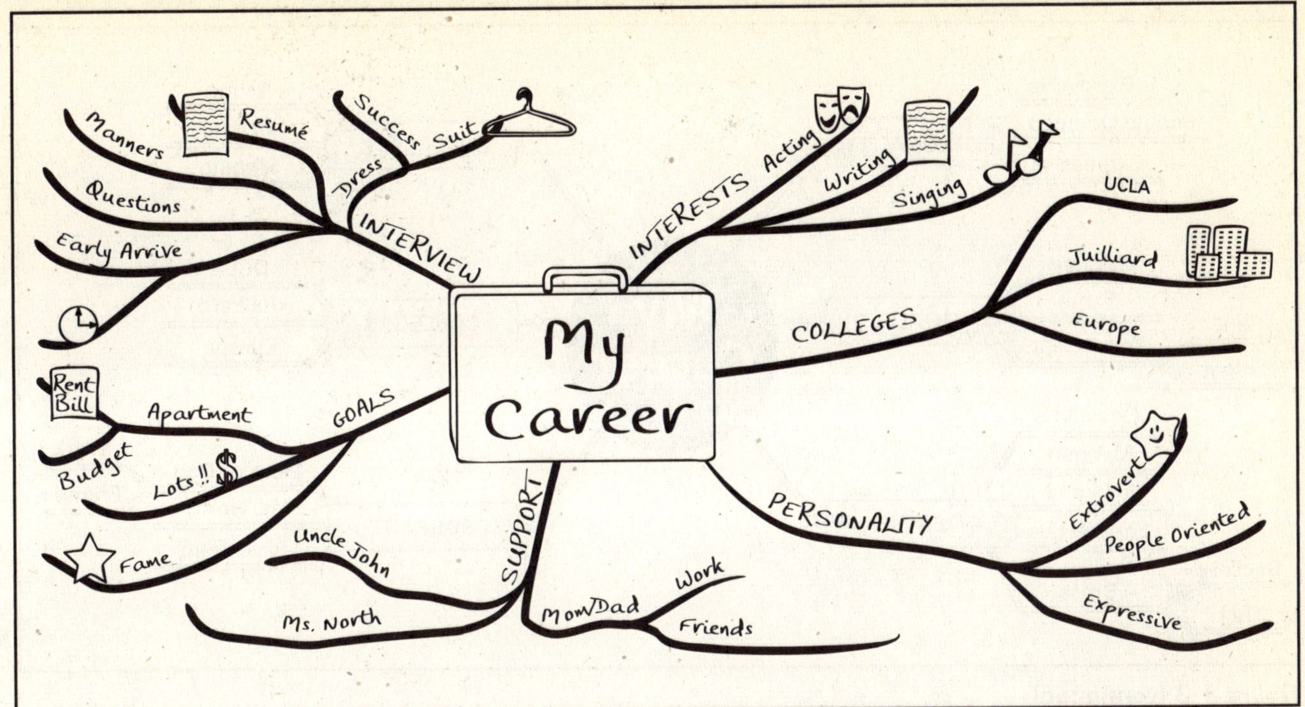

Figure 1-3 Using graphic organizers helps students with disabilities improve their writing skills.

Math in the FACS Classroom

Everyday math is a critical skill. Most recipes require an understanding of basic math while special steps or conversions may require additional explanation. Adding, subtracting, dividing, measuring, conversions, or fractions require solid math skills or access to a calculator so that students can accurately use a recipe or balance a checkbook. The amount of assistance a student may need often varies.

FACS teachers need to reinforce math skills because these skills are used daily. In the kitchen, have students practice using the measuring cups and spoons to see how ¼ cup of oil becomes 1 cup of oil when quadrupling a recipe. Or, eight ounces of cheese becomes a pound when the recipe is doubled. By using the language of science, math, and English in class and showing students the relevance of learning these skills, you can give students the understanding and motivation to strengthen their core academic skills.

Accommodations: Some common accommodations for the math tasks in your classroom follow:

- Provide calculators for students' daily use and during tests.
- Use the buddy system to pair students with other students who have stronger skills.
- Use team projects so a student receives help when it is his or her turn to do math calculations.

The following case study shows how poor math skills are accommodated using the buddy system and technology. Sam uses his strong reading skills as his contribution to the team.

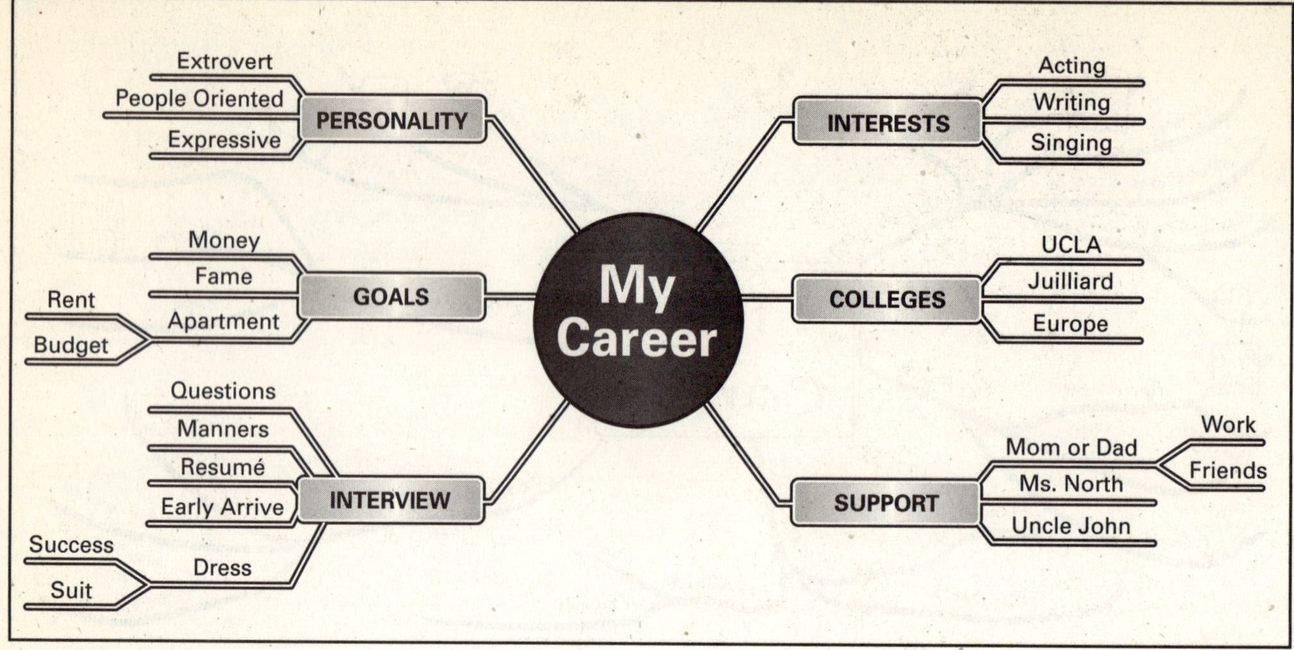

Figure 1-3 (continued)

CASE STUDY

Accommodating Math in Foods Lab

Sam wanted to help his teammates plan a week of healthful meals for a busy family. The team first discussed the family size and age of each member. Next, the team determined which meals involved home cooking or eating out at a restaurant. Determining the nutritional value of the meal required creating food portions and counting calories. The team collected menus from local restaurants and consulted cookbooks. Other team members determined the menus and portion sizes, while Sam, who was not very strong in math, partnered with someone who understood how to enter the data into a nutritional analysis program. Sam discovered the software performed the calculations accurately using formulas. Soon, Sam was entering the data into the software and his partner was checking his work. He had never realized eating out added so many calories to his daily food intake unless he controlled the types of foods he ordered.

Following Up With technology aids in the classroom, Sam and his team were able to see that everyone worked on the project. Sam never felt left out and was able to feel successful.

Summary

Section 1 presented the benefits of the inclusive classroom, government information and statistics definitions, and an overview of FACS content areas with case studies. As a teacher, your expectations help determine the ways that your students will succeed. Your role is pivotal in helping every student become successful.

Take time to notice a student in your room. How does he or she sit in the chair during discussions? Is it the same way he or she sits during silent reading or while taking a test? Does each student sit the same way each day or does it vary? Is the student's expressive language always the same style?

Students tell you a great deal of information with their word choices and body language. Most of the time, they are unaware of how much they are telling you. By observing how a student works within your classroom, you can begin to understand if the student is engaged and if he or she is learning. If you study one student over a two-week timeframe, you can begin to understand his or her reaction to your style of teaching. Try it!

Some famous people with special needs have lived full and successful lives. People with disabilities have become Olympic athletes, actors, authors, public speakers, college professors, sports stars, musicians, comedians, illustrators, U.S. Presidents, and a Miss America winner. See Figure 1-4.

Figure 1-4

Famous Person	Disability	Accomplishments
Jim Abbot	Born without a right hand	1988 Olympic gold winner, pitcher.
Chris Burke	Down Syndrome	Actor from the series, *Life Goes On*, public speaker, author.
Tom Cruise	Dyslexia	Actor.
Patty Duke	Manic-Depressive Disorder, or Bipolar Disorder	Actor, public speaker.
Annette Funicello	Multiple Sclerosis (acquired as an adult)	Actor, one of the original "Mouseketeers" of the Mickey Mouse Club.
Stephen Hawking	Amyotrophic Lateral Sclerosis (ALS) (acquired as an adult)	College professor, author.
Henry Holden	Polio	Actor, public speaker.
Abraham Lincoln	Marfand's Syndrome	16th President of the U.S.
Casey Martin	Kippel-Trenaunay-Weber Syndrome	Golfer.
Terence Parkin	Deaf	2000 Olympic silver medal winner, swimmer.
Itzhak Perlman	Polio	Violinist.
Patricia Polacco	Dyslexia, Dysnumeria, and Dysgraphia	Writer, illustrator.
Christopher Reeve	Spinal cord injury (acquired as an adult)	Actor.
Franklin Roosevelt	Polio	32nd President of the U.S.
Marla Runyan	Blind and Stargardt disease	2000 Olympic competitor, runner.
Mike Utley	Spinal cord injury (acquired as an adult)	NFL star.
Heather Whitestone	Deaf	1995 Miss America.
Stevie Wonder	Retinopathy of Prematurity (ROP—formerly retrolental fibroplasia) (blind)	Singer, musician, and song writer.

Section 2: Meeting the Needs of All Learners

Family and Consumer Sciences (FACS) teachers across the country are teaching a more diverse student population than ever before. Students with disabilities, students who speak English as a second language and language learners, or other at-risk students present new challenges. Many teachers are struggling with how to assure that students learn course objectives and meet the high academic standards and assessments that schools must implement.

One approach to instructional design that has received increasing attention from federal legislators and national leaders is called "Universal Design for Learning," or simply "UDL." According to Skip Stahl, senior associate at the Center for Applied Special Technology (CAST), UDL is an approach to creating course instruction, materials, and content to benefit people of all learning styles and disabilities without adaptation or specialized design. The thrust of UDL is that it makes essential course content accessible to all students by making curricula flexible and customizable. It is important to mention that UDL does not water-down the curricula in any way or adjust academic standards; rather, it allows for essential course content to be taught in multiple ways. Basically, UDL is a new name for an old concept—good teaching.

Good teaching involves sensitivity to the different ways students learn. Teaching and assessment methods that engage the senses and include relaying information visually, auditorally, and kinesthetically tend to produce the best instructional outcomes. In short, making course content accessible to all students, regardless of impairment or learning style, maximizes learning.

What Is UDL?

The term "Universal Design" has its roots in the field of architecture. Architects are mandated by federal legislation and encouraged by best practice to design structures that accommodate the widest spectrum of people. So buildings, parks, and streets are designed with curb cuts, wheelchair ramps, and other accessibility (or barrier-free) features. For example, people of all ages and abilities benefit from curb cuts and ramps as business people pull their luggage through airports and children ride their bikes through neighborhoods. In fact, these more accessible buildings and streets are used and appreciated by persons without disabilities, as much as by people who use assistive mobility devices.

Applied to learning, the concept of Universal Design is extended in two ways:

1. Building an educational curriculum that is flexible to meeting students' diverse needs.
2. Building a curriculum that provides not only access to information, but also access to learning.

The goal of UDL is not to make learning easier for the student or to minimize the effort the student needs to put forth in the classroom. Rather, the goal is to make the curriculum accessible so that students have the opportunity to view, process, and retain information in a variety of ways that maximize their strengths and promote engagement in the learning process.

Three Principles of UDL

To clearly demonstrate these ideas, the Center for Applied Special Technology (CAST) has formulated three basic principles of UDL:

1. **Recognition:** To provide many examples of information in multiple formats and media.
2. **Strategic:** To provide multiple pathways for students to interact with the information and express what they know.
3. **Affective:** To provide multiple ways to engage and motivate students on an intrinsic level.

These three principles, as identified in the book, *Teaching Every Student in the Digital Age: Universal Design for Learning*, written by CAST co-executive directors David H. Rose and Anne Meyer and published by ASCD, are based on three corresponding brain networks.

Recognition Networks

Recognition networks are devoted to pattern recognition—being able to identify basic patterns, such as letters and words, to more complex patterns such as paragraphs, themes, and relationships among concepts. Recognition networks bring cohesion to the information. When you organize vocabulary words by color using red to represent foods, blue to represent food preparation techniques, and yellow to represent equipment, you help your students recognize vocabulary patterns.

Strategic Networks

Strategic brain networks are responsible for knowing how to do things, such as reading a recipe, browning ground meat, making a casserole, or budgeting a trip, etc. Because actions, skills, and plans are highly organized and patterned activities, strategic networks work in conjunction with recognition networks to perform academic tasks, such as writing a weekly meal plan, completing a project, or comparing prices. When teachers require students to learn how to do something, skills and strategies are the focus.

Affective Networks

The affective network is embedded deep in the center of the brain. This network is devoted to emotion and motivation. The affective network is pivotal in engaging and motivating the student to set goals and establish priorities to master the learning objectives. As students receive feedback to validate their understanding of course materials, their self-esteem and confidence increase and they are more willing to persevere when learning becomes more challenging. When teachers select goals or activities that students find relevant and stimulating, affective networks are activated. Students are more likely to learn when *what* they are learning has relevance to their lives. See Figure 2-1.

Learning Involves the Whole Brain

The recognition, strategic, and affective brain networks function together in learning. While some learning may rely more on one network than another, much of learning involves the whole brain as an integrated unit. The three basic principles of UDL tap into these interrelated brain networks. Providing many examples of information in multiple formats allows students to learn content through their preferred way of learning.

Students with disabilities who may have processing disorders or sensory impairments are more likely to gain an understanding of a concept if one of the ways it's presented taps into their strengths. A student who is hearing impaired or has an auditory processing disorder needs to see many examples to learn a concept. If you are teaching students to find recipes, allowing them to use recipe search engines on the Web provides another avenue of access to information in addition to classroom textbooks and cookbooks. For a student with a visual or reading disability, screen reader software can read the Web, making it easier for the student to access the information and meet your class objectives.

In the case study that follows, see how Andrew uses a computer with a screen reader to accommodate his reading disability. Currently in Mrs. Miller's class all students can choose how to find recipes—either using traditional classroom cookbooks or using the Web to find recipes. Until Andrew joined the class, Mrs. Miller only had one way to find recipes—the traditional way. Now the entire class can search the Web for recipes using several recipe search engines.

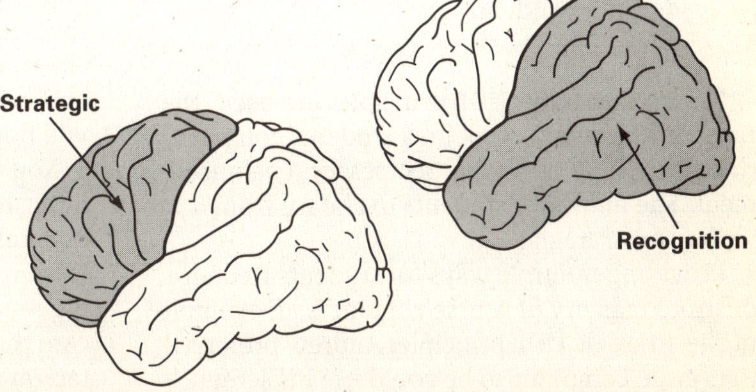

Figure 2-1 The recognition, strategic, and affection networks of the brain work together as students learn.

Case Study

Andrew Uses a Screen Reader

Andrew was diagnosed with dyslexia in elementary school, making it difficult for him to read words. He learned to use a screen reader to read content on the computer. The use of headphones allowed him to hear the screen reader tell what the Web pages said. He learned to use this assistive technology in middle school and has become quite independent with its use.

When Mrs. Miller found out that Andrew was in her class and needed to use computers adapted with screen readers, she decided to talk with Andrew's special education teacher. One of her course objectives stated that "Students will find recipes to prepare a balanced meal." She has a variety of cookbooks for students to use. "How can I change the assignment for just one student?" she thought. After she discussed the problem with Mr. Mackey, the special education teacher, she realized that she didn't need to change the objective. She could let all the students choose to use either the cookbooks or the Web to find recipes.

Andrew used his screen reader to locate recipes on the Web. He found recipes quicker on the Web than his peers could find recipes using the traditional cookbooks. Mrs. Miller decided to let all of her students have the option of using the Web to find recipes.

Following Up In Andrew's case, Mr. Mackey, the special education teacher, worked with Mrs. Miller before the semester started to assure that her classroom computer had the appropriate screen reader software installed. Mr. Mackey also assured Mrs. Miller that Andrew could use his screen reader independently.

Notice that when UDL principles are used, the teacher does not control how students complete the assignment of finding recipes for a balanced meal. She allows *all* students to choose from a variety of strategies.

Providing multiple ways for students to demonstrate mastery of course content is an example of the strategic UDL principle. Andrew preferred to use the computer so he could use his screen reader to accommodate his reading disability. A student with a fine-motor disability who has difficulty writing may prefer to take an oral assessment instead of an assessment that requires writing. Other options include devices such as TestTalker™ or voice-recognition software. When teachers provide multiple means of expression, students are given options and can choose methods that support their interests and skill levels.

Seven Key Strategies of UDL

The three basic principles previously described can be translated into seven recommended strategies for implementing UDL. These strategies integrate the brain's recognition, strategic, and affective networks in the learning process. See Figure 2-2. Each strategy is then discussed in context showing how to implement the strategy within the FACS classroom.

Figure 2-2

Seven Key Strategies of UDL

1. Create a classroom climate that fosters trust and respect.
2. Identify the essential course content.
3. Clearly express the essential content and any feedback given to the student.
4. Integrate natural support for learning.
5. Use a variety of instructional methods.
6. Allow multiple methods of demonstrating understanding of essential course content.
7. Use technology to increase accessibility.

Strategy 1: Create a Classroom Climate That Fosters Trust and Respect

Teachers can create a climate that fosters trust and respect by openly discussing the expectation that students will respect you, each other, and classroom materials. Disrespectful tones of voice and mocking of students' behavior or projects will not be tolerated.

You can develop a course outline that clearly indicates the course objectives, assignments with due dates, grading scales, and course policies. Within the course objectives, policies, and grading sections of your course outline, clearly indicate that respect is an essential skill that will be taught and graded. Openly discuss how respect will be graded with your students. The course outline serves as a contract between you and the student, outlining expectations and requirements for successful course completion.

As you teach your students how "respect" is demonstrated within your classroom, provide role-plays or examples of respectful interactions. See how Mrs. Randall taught students how to be respectful in the following case study.

Case Study

Students Learn How to Be Respectful

Mrs. Randall knew that behaving in a respectful manner is one of the core FACS objectives. Teaching respect is a continuous process throughout the semester. She set the stage for teaching the students what "respect" really means when she began the first class of the semester with a discussion about class guidelines. Together, she and her students brainstormed their class guidelines. Mrs. Randall knew that respect would appear on the list. See the guidelines the foods class students developed:

1. Respect each other.
2. Be prepared for class.
3. Communicate appropriately.
4. Work together.
5. Apply yourself.
6. Have fun and learn a lot.

Then Mrs. Randall used role-plays to teach multiple examples of respectful comments and tones of voice. She indicated that disrespectful behavior would not be acceptable.

Following Up By using multiple examples of positive, respectful attitudes, comments, and tones of voice, Mrs. Randall made it clear that only these types of behaviors would be tolerated in her classroom. Disrespect would not be accepted and any student who displayed disrespectful behavior would face some type of consequence.

Strategy 2: Identify the Essential Course Content

The most challenging aspect of designing a course is to determine exactly what you want the students to achieve by the end of the course. *Bloom's Taxonomy* provides a useful structure to organize course objectives and assignments to assure that all students are learning competencies across the six categories of the Cognitive Domain. Examples of the skills demonstrated for each category follow.

1. **Knowledge:** Recognize and recall information using such terms as list, define, identify, who, and when.
2. **Comprehension:** Interpret facts and grasp meanings using terms such as explain, infer, or summarize.
3. **Application:** Use information and solve problems in new ways through demonstrations, calculations, and projects.
4. **Analysis:** Recognize patterns or component parts by ordering, inferring, classifying, connecting, and/or arranging concepts.
5. **Synthesis:** Use old ideas to create new ideas by integrating, modifying, and rearranging concepts.
6. **Evaluation:** Assess the value of material based on definite criteria by contrasting, interpreting, and drawing conclusions supported by data.

Balancing course content across the Cognitive Domain and across the recognition, strategic, and affective networks assists teachers in developing courses that are universally designed. The knowledge and comprehension categories require students to use the recognition and strategic UDL networks. The affective UDL network is activated by designing assignments and evaluation activities that provide choice and an adjustable level of challenge for students. This will help students engage in learning and ultimately maximize achievement.

Strategy 3: Clearly Express the Essential Content and Any Feedback Given to the Student

Teachers can clearly identify the essential course content in the course outline in a print-based and/or on-line format, review the course content verbally during the first class session, and clarify the learning objectives and assignments in subsequent class sessions. However, some students may miss the essential content because of numerous reasons including, but not limited to, a hearing-processing disorder, a language barrier, or Attention Deficit Disorder (ADD).

There are several classroom procedures that teachers can implement to assure that students have numerous opportunities to gain the essential course content. For example:

- Give students lesson organizers in advance so they know what will be presented and when they will use the information. This approach motivates students to engage more intently.
- Enhance learning by establishing a time for students to make flash cards of key vocabulary terms and build weekly reviews for students to study with a peer.

When you ask students to graph their progress on self-monitoring charts, you can help build students' self-esteem as they see their progress. Notice how Mei Yang has graphed her progress on a self-monitoring chart. See Figure 2-3.

Quick Facts

Teaching and Learning Styles

Teachers who use a variety of teaching styles make it easier for students to learn. The following list describes common learning styles and the types of teaching best suited to these styles:

- **Auditory Learners:** Students who learn best through hearing lectures and class discussions.
- **Visual Learners:** Students who learn best by seeing such things as charts, graphs, videos, and demonstrations.
- **Kinesthetic Learners:** Students who learn through action such as the doing and touching involved in making a project.

Most students learn through several teaching styles. Teachers who present critical information in a variety of styles are best able to meet the needs of a diverse class of students.

Figure 2-3

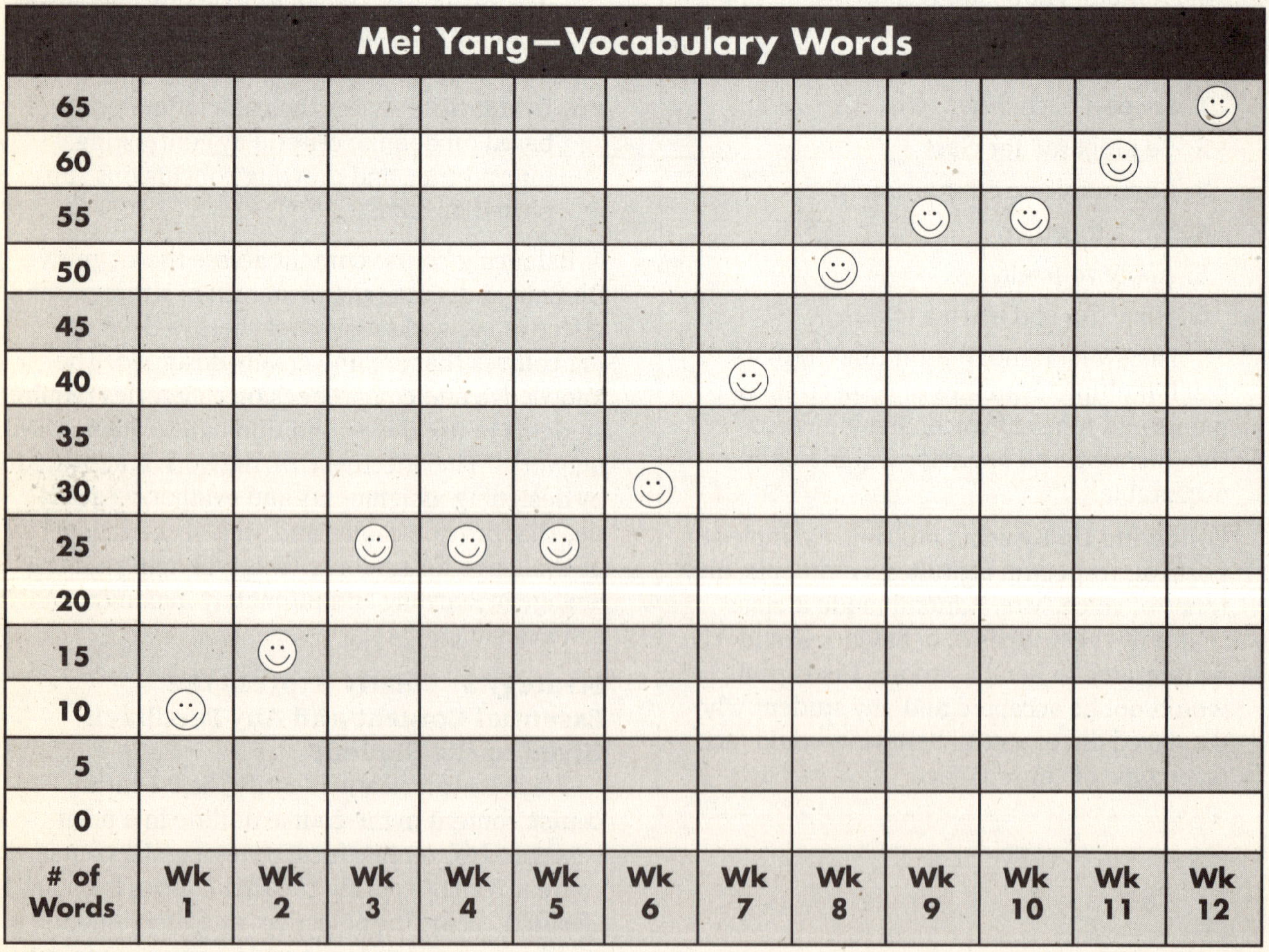

Mei Yang—Vocabulary Words

# of Words	Wk 1	Wk 2	Wk 3	Wk 4	Wk 5	Wk 6	Wk 7	Wk 8	Wk 9	Wk 10	Wk 11	Wk 12
65												☺
60											☺	
55									☺	☺		
50								☺				
45												
40							☺					
35												
30						☺						
25			☺	☺	☺							
20												
15		☺										
10	☺											
5												
0												

Mei's chart shows the number of vocabulary words that she has mastered during peer tutoring each week.

A third method that has empirical evidence for improving classroom performance is the use of guided notes. According to Bill Heward, Professor at Ohio State University, guided notes are instructor-prepared handouts that provide all students with background information and standard cues with specific spaces to write key facts, concepts, and/or relationships during a lecture. This enables students to listen for essential content without copying all the points off the overhead, board, or PowerPoint® slide.

Guided notes require students to actively respond during the lecture, improve the accuracy and efficiency of students' note-taking, and increase students' retention of course content. These handouts can help organize and enhance lecture content in any discipline or subject area.

Lecturing is one of the most common teaching methods used in the classroom because it is versatile and efficiently uses a teacher's time. However, the lecture method also presents some challenges to students who may be passive learners, who are not auditory learners, and who are poor note-takers. Guided notes also help teachers stay organized. By creating guided notes that outline the essential points you want students to learn, you can assure that students gain the essential content. See Figure 2-4.

Strategy 4: Integrate Natural Support for Learning

Teachers can integrate many natural supports within the classroom to enhance the teaching-learning process. Peer mentoring, cooperative learning, and students sharing and discussing their notes in small groups are all strategies to integrate natural support for learning. In many situations, student-to-student interactions are a

Figure 2-4

Guided Notes—Techniques for Mixing Foods

Note: ***Boldface italic*** type shows parts completed by student during the lecture. In the handout passed out to students, the underline would be blank. Students are instructed to fill in the term as the teacher presents the information or describes/demonstrates each technique.

Techniques

1. ***Beat, Combine, Blend*** To thoroughly incorporate one ingredient into another, using a spoon, wire whisk, rotary beater, electric mixer, or electric blender.
2. ***Beat*** To thoroughly mix foods using a vigorous over-and-over motion. Egg whites may be beaten to add air to them.
3. ***Stir*** To mix by hand, using a spoon or wire whisk in a circular motion. Can also be done while cooking to keep food from sticking to the pan and to distribute heat throughout foods.
4. ***Cream*** To beat together ingredients, such as shortening and sugar, until soft and creamy.
5. ***Whip*** To incorporate air into a mixture to make it light and fluffy. Cream may be whipped to make it light and stiff for a topping.
6. ***Fold*** A technique used to gently mix delicate ingredients, usually with a rubber scraper or spoon.

Note: The classroom teacher can prepare guided notes by typing the definitions, then copying the file and eliminating the term. The student version has the blanks. The teacher version could be used as an overhead transparency or PowerPoint® slide.

more effective teaching tool than even the most dynamic lecture. Offering a choice of the type of product to produce engages the affective networks of learning, ultimately increasing the student's motivation to achieve.

Teachers can structure both in-class and out-of-class activities as natural supports for learning. Guided notes can be a catalyst for increasing students' interaction with the essential course content. Encouraging students to select a study buddy for quizzes and developing study guides of course material are all strategies that encourage students to interact with the learning objectives of the course.

Strategy 5: Use a Variety of Instructional Methods

As educators learn more about the teaching-learning process, they realize that learning is very individualized; therefore, educators need to use many different instructional methods to assure that they reach *all* students. Earlier it was discussed that successful teaching and learning requires the interaction of three neural systems: recognition, strategic, and affective. However, while certain instructional methods are more appropriate to teach students to recognize patterns (recognition networks), other methods are better suited for teaching students skills (strategic networks). Still other techniques are preferred to enhance student engagement with the content (affective networks). See Figures 2-5 and 2-6.

Figure 2-5 Students often find it challenging to learn the delicate balance between self, work, and family.

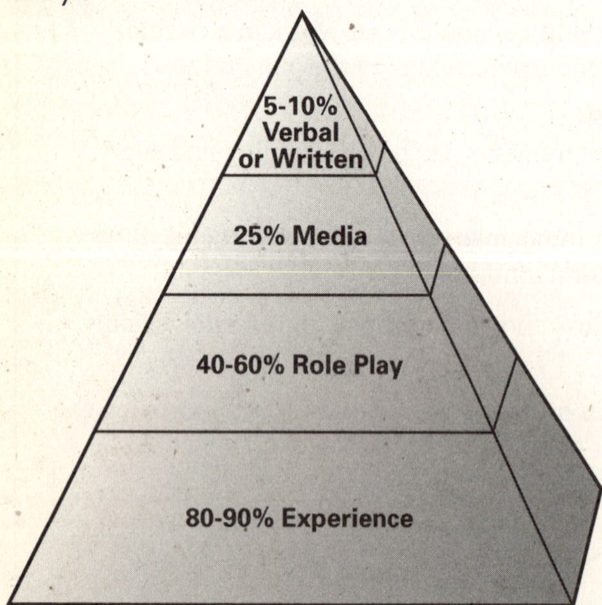

Figure 2-6 on instructional methods (pages 27 and 28) provides a variety of strategies and examples for teaching that are organized by the three neural networks: recognition, strategic, and affective. Review this table when you are teaching new concepts (recognition), skills (strategic), or when you want to increase student motivation for learning (affective).

Recognition: To assist students in recognizing the patterns of essential course content, five strategies are suggested:

1. Provide multiple examples of a concept.
2. Contrast examples with non-examples.
3. Highlight salient points.
4. Present information in multiple formats via technology or multimedia.
5. Support background context by showing how new concepts relate to old concepts.

Strategic: To further enhance strategic learning, four instructional strategies are suggested:

1. Provide flexible models of skilled performance. An example would be actually sautéing vegetables for an Asian dish in a wok.
2. Provide opportunities to practice with supports.
3. Provide ongoing, relevant feedback.
4. Offer students flexible opportunities for demonstrating their skills.

By incorporating peer mentoring, group discussions, and cooperative learning opportunities into teaching, teachers can create numerous opportunities for students to observe skilled performances, practice their skills, and gain relevant feedback. During the acquisition stage of learning, it is critical that students receive continuous feedback on their accuracy to avoid practicing errors. Once students have mastered a skill, they can maintain that skill with an occasional reinforcement activity.

Affective: Feedback and student-to-student interaction, as indicated earlier, also engages affective networks, targeting the emotional and motivational components of learning. Three other recommended methods to support the affective network include:

Figure 2-6

Instructional Methods by Neural System		
Neural Network	**Instructional Methods**	**Examples**
Recognition	Provide multiple examples of a concept.	• Use text in conjunction with pictures, diagrams, photos, definitions, contrast, metaphor, and visual models.
	Contrast examples with non-examples.	• Show students pictures of properly baked products with pictures of baked products that are burned or poorly mixed.
	Highlight similar characteristics of salient points.	• Use voice tone, volume and pitch, body language, expressions, large font, italics, bolded text, icons, and repetition of main points.
	Present information in multiple formats via technology or multimedia.	• Use multimedia representations, such as video, graphs, text, audio, or kinesthetic exercises.
	Support background context by showing how new concepts relate to old concepts.	• Use graphic organizers to contrast similarities with non-examples and provide a context of how the concepts are related.
Strategic	Provide flexible models of skilled performance.	• Use multiple testing modes (e.g., oral reports, demonstrations of skills, projects, written papers, or portfolios), Web-based exercises, kinesthetic lab experiences, out-of-class study or recitation sessions, expert testimonials through video teleconferencing, and Web-based broadcasts.
	Provide opportunities to practice with supports.	• Use study buddies, flash cards, peer mentoring, group discussions, or cooperative learning to provide opportunities for students to practice and demonstrate what they are learning.
	Provide ongoing, relevant feedback.	• Use e-mail, simulations (with or without computers), video recordings of a student's performance, word processing software with "tracking changes," or embedded editorial comments to provide constructive critiques.
	Offer flexible opportunities for demonstrating the skill.	• Use simulations (with or without technology), group demonstrations, and enrichment activities for those who want more practice. For example, when teaching budgeting, allow students to select the type of budget they are proposing (e.g., purchase and maintain a car, rent and furnish an apartment, or budget weekly groceries for a family of three).

Figure 2-6 (continued)

Instructional Methods by Neural System (continued)		
Neural Network	**Instructional Methods**	**Examples**
Affective	Allow student-to-student interaction and peer feedback targeting the emotional and motivational components of learning.	• Use peer mentoring, cooperative learning, and student selection of projects or topic areas of personal interest that have relevance.
	Offer students choice in course content and tools.	• Give students a choice of assignments, including assignments that involve technology mediums, such as: PowerPoint®, Web articles, and Web page design. • Offer students a choice of software programs to complete assignments (e.g., Microsoft Word®, PowerPoint®, Excel®, Inspiration®, or assistive technology programs, such as Kurzweil® or Wynn®). • Provide students with a choice of communication mediums (e.g., e-mail, phone, chat, discussion boards, and instant messaging).
	Challenge students, but not beyond their individual reach.	• Offer students assignments that include basic recall as well as critical thinking skills. • Provide students ample opportunity to give feedback about the course throughout the semester via in-class discussion, e-mail dialogue, electronic or hard-copy surveys, discussion boards, etc. • Instruct students in a manner in which they do not have the opportunity to lose interest; however, pace instruction so that students are not overwhelmed.
	Offer choice of learning contexts.	• Offer students a choice of assignment formats (e.g., in-class assignment, homework, small/large group discussions). • Offer students a choice in how they deliver a presentation. Lessons can be structured into games with teams and virtual points.

1. Offer students choices in how they demonstrate mastery of course content by letting them choose to complete a related project, take a test, or demonstrate their skills.
2. Challenge a student, but not beyond his or her individual reach.
3. Offer a choice of learning contexts (in-class assignment, homework, small/large group discussion, multi-media, etc.).

For example, a teacher may give a student a choice in how he or she delivers a presentation, or the teacher may structure a rote memorization lesson into a game with teams and virtual points, such as modified versions of television game shows to fit course content. Ultimately, empowering students to make decisions and offering out-of-the ordinary, fun activities can yield higher engagement and emotional investment in learning outcomes.

Strategy 6: Allow Multiple Methods of Demonstrating Understanding of Essential Course Content

Providing flexibility and opportunities for student choice in how they will be assessed and how they will demonstrate knowledge is an excellent way to increase students' enthusiasm for learning. Building that type of choice into a course allows students to express mastery of course content in multiple ways. For example, without compromising academic rigor, completing an oral presentation instead of a written paper may provide a student with the motivation to expend the extra energy needed to learn the essential content.

Multiple methods of demonstrating knowledge of course content may have particular relevance for students with disabilities. Allowing students to use an alternate means of assessment, and time to complete the assessment, gives them a chance to demonstrate what they know based on their strengths. For instance, if a student has a processing disorder such as dyslexia, then using a written assessment may be counterproductive. The student may know all the course content, but cannot demonstrate what he or she knows adequately through reading and writing. In this situation, an oral assessment, a demonstration, or a project may be more appropriate to assess student learning.

Strategy 7: Use Technology to Increase Accessibility

Technology is a useful tool for creating maximum access to course content. For example, putting the course outline on-line allows students with visual impairments to use assistive technologies, such as screen readers or magnifiers. Students with learning disabilities can use text-to-speech software programs so they can hear the course outline information and process it aurally as opposed to visually. The Web can be a powerful tool for increasing access and meeting students' diverse learning needs, especially when principles of Web accessibility are employed.

However, to only view technology and Universal Design in the context of disability limits the widespread impact of digital media. Here are some ways that digital media can benefit all students:

- Closed captioning can help a student who relies on English as a second language and language learners as well as a person with a hearing impairment or impaired auditory processing.
- Scanning material from hard copy to digital form can also be useful for students with various disabilities and students who use English as a second language and language learners because it allows for editing and formatting consistent with learning strengths and strategies.
- Word processing programs benefit all students because they provide a means of greater organization and prioritization of learning along with increased visual access to the text. You can use these programs to enlarge the font in course handouts or to highlight critical ideas.

All these examples are simple yet effective ways teachers can use technology to build bridges to learning.

Summary

The increasing diversity of students in today's schools calls for greater flexibility in instructional design if teachers are to teach effectively. To help meet the vast learning needs of students, Universal Design for Learning (UDL) has the potential to reach a wider range of students and to produce better learning outcomes. By providing multiple representations of information, multiple means of expression, and multiple means of engagement, teachers can create a versatile teaching approach that is sensitive to all students' abilities and learning strengths. Depending on the disability, some students with special needs may need further accommodations and adaptations.

Across the country, educators are implementing UDL strategies to offer the best possible education for their students. Although program names may vary from district to district and state to state, the core strategies of UDL, or good teaching, remain the same. For more information regarding how the principles of UDL are implemented in your area, contact your local, regional, or state education departments.

Section 3: Special Education Policies and Practices

Family and Consumer Sciences (FACS) teachers attend Individualized Education Program (IEP) meetings for special education students with increasing regularity. These meetings are an opportunity for a team of educators, parents, and involved personnel to design an appropriate educational program to meet the special learning needs of a student. In this section you will learn about:

- Federal laws that guide the education of students with disabilities.
- The IEP process.
- The importance of the FACS teacher in the educational programs for students with disabilities.

Laws Guarantee Services

Four federal laws guarantee the rights of persons with disabilities. These laws include:

- The Individuals with Disabilities Act (IDEA) of 1997.
- Section 504 of the Rehabilitation Act of 1973.
- No Child Left Behind Act of 2001.
- Americans with Disabilities Act of 1990.

The current law governing special education services for students with disabilities is IDEA. The current law governing elementary and secondary schools is the No Child Left Behind Act (NCLB) of 2001. Both IDEA and NCLB emphasize the need for higher academic standards, including those for students with disabilities. The IDEA law emphasizes the need for higher academic standards. IDEA mandates that the IEP for students with disabilities include a statement indicating how the student's disability affects his or her involvement and progress in the general curricula. At the IEP meeting, teachers can share with the student, parents, and others on the IEP team how the student is progressing in their classes. Each of these laws is discussed in the order of importance to school-age students with disabilities.

IDEA Specifics

IDEA guarantees special education and related services to eligible students with disabilities who are 3 to 21 years of age and who have disabilities that affect learning. Some states offer services beyond IDEA requirements. The six major principles of IDEA are:

- **Child Find System:** Each state is responsible for locating, evaluating, and identifying all students with disabilities who will benefit from special education services. If you suspect a student may have a disability, talk with either your principal or the special educator in your school.
- **Protection in Evaluation Procedures:** Schools must use nondiscriminatory testing and a multifactored approach in gathering information to determine eligibility for special education services. You may be invited to participate in a Multifactored Evaluation team meeting (MFE). If you are invited, you will be providing information to determine if the student has a disability and what appropriate services may benefit the student.
- **Free and Appropriate Public Education (FAPE):** An Individualized Education Program (IEP) is required for each student with a disability who qualifies for special education services. Students with disabilities have the right to a FAPE through age 21 or high school graduation, whichever comes first. If you are invited to an IEP meeting, you will be helping design appropriate specialized services, including annual goals and short-term objectives.
- **Least Restrictive Environment:** IDEA promotes inclusion in the traditional classroom. Since so much of FACS curricula relates to independent living skills, the FACS classroom is an ideal learning environment for many students with disabilities.
- **Due Process Safeguards:** Schools must provide protection for the rights of each student and their parents.

- **Student and Parent Cooperative Decision Making:** Schools must include input from both the parents and the students in designing and implementing services.

Section 504 of the Rehabilitation Act

Section 504 of the Rehabilitation Act of 1973 protects the rights of people with disabilities in school or work settings. Under this law no one may keep a student with a disability from participating in a program that receives money from the federal government simply because he or she has a disability. For example, a student with disabilities may not be excluded from school or class because an accessibility or appropriate accommodation is unavailable. Accessibility to classes might mean that a subject is taught in a different classroom so a student who uses a wheelchair may attend the class.

For students to receive services under Section 504, they must identify their disability and needed accommodations. Your school administrator will develop a 504 Plan with the student. A 504 Plan is different from an IEP plan in that it only addresses the need for accommodations and does not address specially designed instruction.

No Child Left Behind Act

The No Child Left Behind Act (NCLB) of 2001 was designed to improve student achievement. NCLB mandates:

- Strong academic standards for reading, math, and science.
- Assessments that lead annual district and state reports showing results for designated groups of students, including those with disabilities.

This level of accountability has focused national attention on raising the quality of education.

Americans with Disabilities Act

The Americans with Disabilities Act (ADA) covers everyone with a disability, regardless of age. Under the ADA, no one may discriminate against a person with a disability across three broad areas: employment, public services, and education, including postsecondary institutions. The ADA protects many of the same rights as are protected under Section 504. See the ADA Web site on the Internet for more information.

The IEP Process

The IEP team meets annually to assess a student's progress, review a student's vision for his or her future, and determine what services and supports are needed to prepare the student to be successful and reach his or her potential.

According to IDEA, certain people should be involved in writing the IEP. They include:

- The student (when appropriate).
- Parents and/or guardians of the student.
- At least one general education teacher.
- At least one of the special education teachers.
- A professional that interprets the test results.
- A representative of the school system.
- Representatives from other agencies who may be providing transition services, such as rehabilitation counselors, service coordinators, or employment specialists.

The IEP team designs education and transition services that promote movement from high school to adult settings such as college, employment, and independent living. In the case study that follows, see how Mrs. Morris realized the benefits of her participation in IEP meetings to her students, their parents, and future service coordinators such as rehabilitation counselors.

Case Study

Focusing the IEP on What's Important: Respect, Cooperation, and Meeting Objectives

At first, Mrs. Morris felt intimidated going to IEP meetings. They always used so many acronyms that she really didn't understand what the team members were talking about. Things like IEP, MFE, SLD, and PLOP... sounded like a different language. Then she realized that so often special education students were more successful in her classes than in more traditional classes such as English and math. Her special education students earned "A's" and "B's" in her classes because she valued and graded daily participation, respect, and cooperation, as well as test scores. The quizzes only counted for 20 percent of the students' grades. It was more important to produce quality work each day and work cooperatively together than it was to "ACE" the weekly quiz. Both students and parents were often surprised to see an 'A' on the report card for her classes.

Mrs. Morris remembered talking to Sally and Mrs. Parker at Sally's IEP meeting. Mrs. Parker said, "Thank you so much for giving Sally an 'A' in Consumer Education." When I told her that Sally earned every point of that "A," and that I wished all my students brought Sally's cooperative attitude to class, Mrs. Parker's eyes began to water. As she held back her tears, I realized that not many teachers had complimented Sally for the strengths that she brought to class each day. Unfortunately, a few of her other teachers were always frustrated because Sally learned slowly and received poor grades on the tests. They were concerned because Sally was always bringing down the class average. Both the special educator and the principal reinforced Sally's excellent social and employability skills. The rehabilitation counselor stated that with such great work skills, Sally would be able to get a job in the community, instead of the sheltered workshop.

Following Up After Sally's meeting, Mrs. Morris went to every IEP meeting for her special education students with a positive attitude. If she could help focus the IEP on the student's strengths, and staff members could begin to work together to build on these strengths, then often the student and parents would have hope that the student could become productively employed in the community.

The Annual IEP Meeting

Although every IEP meeting is different, most meetings follow a similar pattern. Currently more students are becoming actively involved in the meeting (especially those in high school). Since the student is one person that knows the majority of the people in the room, he or she can be responsible for introductions. Since this fits within many FACS curricula, you could help the student to practice making appropriate introductions so the student introduces you to his or her parents, the special education teacher, and other IEP team members.

Although actual forms may vary from state to state, by law, the IEP must include the following information about the student and the program that is designed to meet the student's needs in promoting movement to productive transition adult roles.

Present Level of Performance: A description of how the student is doing in school (academically and socially) and how the disability affects his or her progress in the general curricula.

Annual Goals: Goal statements that describe what the student will achieve during the next year that will promote his or her movement toward future plans.

Short-term Objectives: A description of how each goal is broken down into short-term measurable objectives.

Special Education and Related Services: A list of the special education and related services (e.g., speech, transportation, and work-study services) that will be provided along with the days and times that students receive the services.

Participating with Non-disabled Students: The extent, if any, to which the student will participate with students who do not have disabilities.

Participation in State and District-wide Tests: The accommodations students will need to take achievement tests given by your state or district.

Dates and Places: When services will begin, how often they will be provided, where they will be provided, and how long they will last.

Transition Service Needs: The courses the student will need to take to reach his or her goals for life after high school, including a statement of the student's needs for transition services.

Transition Services: Beginning at 16 years of age (or younger, if appropriate), a statement of the transition services the student will need to help him or her prepare to leave high school.

Age of Majority Statement: One year before the student reaches the age of majority (age 18 in most states), a student must be provided with a written document stating the rights that will transfer from the parents or guardians to the student when he or she reaches that age.

Measuring Progress: The student's progress will be measured by the goals and objectives that are met. This information is shared at the annual IEP meeting when new goals and objectives are established for the upcoming year.

Teachers and the IEP team work together to set up a plan to help the student to be successful both in school and in the years following high school. By actively involving the student in the meeting, he or she has the opportunity to learn important skills about relating to others, negotiating supports and services, and planning for future events. See Figure 3-1.

Figure 3-1

Sequence of an IEP Meeting

1. Introduce the IEP team members.
2. Review the agenda for the meeting.
3. Discuss the student's vision for the future (e.g., college and employment options).
4. Discuss the student's career and independent living interests, preferences, strengths, and challenges. (Often referred to as the *Present Level of Performance*—PLOP.)
5. Review the past year by discussing last year's IEP and comparing last year's vision with your current plans for the future. Discuss why changes have occurred, why goals have not been met, and celebrate any goal or objective that has been accomplished.
6. Discuss what the student wants to achieve this year. Ask the student, his or her parents, and the other participants what goals, objectives, and services should be considered.
7. Review services that may be available from other agencies such as rehabilitation services, mental health agencies, employment agencies, and/or other community-based agencies.
8. Recommend goals and objectives for the upcoming year.
9. Discuss needed accommodations for any assessment requirements such as extended time, distraction-free and/or alternative testing settings, assistive technology, readers, scribes, note-takers, etc.
10. Negotiate specific recommendations for services and supports that the student needs to accomplish his or her goals.
11. Discuss who will maintain records to monitor progress of goals, objectives, timelines, and responsibilities of each team member.
12. Agree on a date for the next meeting and when each member will get copies of the final IEP for the current year. If an IEP team member was not able to attend, discuss who will share the results of the meeting with that member.

The FACS Teacher's Role

You have an important role in planning and delivering quality education programs for students with disabilities. FACS courses on independent living, food and fitness, life skills, personal and career development, and child development and parenting all have learning objectives that are relevant to all students.

When you attend IEP meetings, you gain an understanding of the specialized instruction or accommodations that each student needs to learn best. For example, if a student learns best when another student takes notes for him or her during a lecture so he or she can focus on content and not on the note-taking process, then you will know the steps that you can take to support this student. By being involved in the IEP meeting, you have an opportunity to participate in the discussion and determine how to implement accommodations and supports in your classroom.

Special education services work best when everyone works together as a team. The student and his or her parents set the long-range vision for the future—whether it is college, employment, or some combination of these post-school outcomes. The special educator reviews the present level of performance (PLOP) and helps the IEP team determine the goals and objectives that need to be accomplished to promote movement towards the student's long-range vision. The FACS teacher delivers the independent living skills the student will need to know to be successful in his or her long-range vision. The transition specialist coordinates transition and work-study services so the student can earn credit while working at a paid job in his or her vocational area of interest. When the team communicates and supports each other, students receive quality educational services.

FACS teachers may participate in the design, delivery, and evaluation of special education services in the following ways:

- **Make every effort to accommodate individual students' needs.** FACS teachers must make an effort to be flexible in adapting, accommodating, or modifying the curricula so an appropriate education is delivered to every student.
- **Evaluate academic abilities in accordance with guidelines provided through the IEP and/or recommendations from the special educator.** FACS teachers must be able to report specifically and precisely how students can or cannot perform in all academic areas addressed in the FACS classroom.
- **If you suspect that a student may have a disability but is not receiving services, discuss your concerns about the student's performance with the administrator responsible for special education services in your school.** A referral to special education services is justified only if a number of teaching strategies have been tried and failed. Most students receiving special education services have been identified in elementary or middle school.
- **Participate in eligibility conferences if invited.** Before a student is provided special education services, his or her eligibility for services must be determined by an interdisciplinary team. You may be asked to participate on this team and to describe how the student performs in your class. You will need to state if you believe the student has a disability and will benefit from special education services.
- **Participate in writing the IEP.** During an IEP team meeting, an appropriate educational program is designed. Come to this meeting with goals and objectives that the student needs to accomplish his or her long-range vision.
- **Communicate with parents or guardians.** FACS teachers must communicate with the student's parents or guardians on the progress the student is making in class and on the IEP goals that are being implemented in class.
- **Participate in due process hearings.** A due process hearing is held when parents, students, or teachers are dissatisfied with the school's response to the student's educational needs. You may be called on to offer opinions, observations, or suggestions in such hearings.
- **Collaborate with other professionals in identifying and making maximum use of exceptional students' abilities.** FACS and special education teachers are expected to work together and share responsibility for educating students with special needs. You should meet with your special education colleagues regarding the progress of students with disabilities in your classes. See Figure 3-2 on page 35.

Figure 3-2

Special Education: Common Acronyms and Their Meanings	
ADD	Attention Deficit Disorder
ADHD	Attention Deficit/Hyperactivity Disorder
ASD	Autism Spectrum Disorder
BD	Behavior Disorder
DTH	Day Training and Habilitation
ED	Emotionally Disturbed (also referred to as emotional disturbance)
EBD	Emotional and Behavior Disorder
ESY	Extended School Year
FAPE	Free and Appropriate Public Education
FAS	Fetal Alcohol Syndrome
HI	Hearing Impairment
IDEA	Individuals with Disabilities Education Act
IEE	Independent Educational Evaluation
IEP	Individualized Education Program
LD	Learning Disabled
LEA	Local Education Agency
LRE	Least Restrictive Environment
MFE	Multifactored Evaluation
MR	Mental Retardation
OHI	Other Health Impairments
OI	Orthopedic Impairments
PAS	Personal Attendant Services
PCA	Personal Care Attendants
PLOP	Present Level of Performance
SLD	Specific Learning Disability
TBI	Traumatic Brain Injury
SSI	Supplemental Security Insurance
VI	Visual Impairment

*Although it does not fit special education guidelines, ELL (English Language Learners) has been added as an acronym to the accommodations and modifications in the activity plans of this booklet.

Summary

The FACS teacher has an important role in educating students with disabilities. Both the curricula and teaching style within FACS programs are a good match to what many students with disabilities need. Although special education terminology can be confusing at first, you can make a significant contribution to the quality of life of students with disabilities. For additional information on your role in educating students with specific disabilities, see *Sections 4*, *5*, and *6*.

Section 4: Teaching Students with Invisible Disabilities

According to the U.S. Department of Education, approximately 50 percent of all students receiving special education services have invisible disabilities. For example, students with learning disabilities, Attention Deficit Disorder (ADD), Attention Deficit/Hyperactivity Disorder (ADHD), or emotional disturbances may be receiving special education services, supports, and accommodations even though they do not appear to have a disability. There are numerous other invisible disabilities such as heart conditions, Chronic Fatigue Syndrome, Juvenile Fibromyalgia, and Seizure Disorder. The severity of students' functional limitations does not depend on your personal ability to see the disability.

There may be several students in your classroom with invisible disabilities. Of these students, some may receive accommodations such as extended time on assessments or study aids such as guided notes. Other students may have behavioral contracts to increase or decrease certain targeted behaviors. For those students who receive accommodations, services, or support, it is important to collaborate with the student and special education staff to meet the needs of the student. If you would like to know more about students with invisible disabilities than is provided in this section, ask the special educators in your school or refer to the resources listed in *Section 9*.

Learning Disabilities

A specific learning disability is defined as a disorder in one or more of the basic psychological processes involved in understanding or in using language—spoken or written—which may manifest itself in an imperfect ability to listen, think, speak, read, write, spell, or to do mathematical calculations. The term includes conditions, such as perceptual handicaps, brain injury, minimal brain dysfunction, dyslexia, and developmental aphasia. The term does not include children who have learning problems that are primarily the result of visual, hearing, or motor disabilities; of cognitive impairment/mental retardation; or of environmental, cultural, or economic disadvantages.

Students with learning disabilities often learn differently than their peers. Although they often have average or above average intelligence, there is frequently a discrepancy between their abilities and their achievements in specific areas due to a central nervous system dysfunction. A learning disability is a permanent disorder that interferes with integrating, acquiring, or demonstrating verbal or nonverbal abilities and skills. Frequently, there are some processing or memory deficits as well.

Common Learning Disabilities

Students with learning disabilities may have difficulties with one or more of the following:

- Reading comprehension.
- Mathematics.
- Oral expression.
- Written expression.
- Auditory processing.
- Visual processing.
- Abstract reasoning.
- Visual spatial skills.
- Processing speed.

Keep in mind that one person doesn't have difficulty with all of the above-mentioned areas. Also, it is not unusual for people with learning disabilities to be gifted in some areas.

Students with learning disabilities experience a wide range of learning, social, and emotional problems. Each student with a learning disability may need different types of accommodations, services, or support based on what area of learning is affected by the disability.

Teaching Suggestions and Common Accommodations for Students with Learning Disabilities

In addition to the teaching suggestions presented in *Section 2, Meeting the Needs of All Learners*, students with learning disabilities may also benefit from the following suggestions.

Supportive Environment: At the beginning of the course announce that you are willing to provide accommodations for all students. Meet individually with students who are having difficulty. You should ask:

- "In what ways can I help you understand the material we cover in class?"
- "Can we work together to brainstorm some possible solutions for difficulties you might have with this class?"
- "How have other teachers helped you learn?"

Teaching Style: Provide important information and assignments in both oral and written formats to help promote students' understanding by hearing and seeing content. Using a variety of teaching styles to present information assists students in learning that is consistent with their preferred learning styles.

Reading Assignments: Decrease the amount of required reading by providing summaries of important concepts.

Peer Teams: Allow students to work in pairs or small groups for cooperative learning. Select groupings based upon students' strengths.

Technology: Allow students to use technology to support the learning effort. Examples include Personal Digital Assistants (PDAs), computers, or spell checkers. Use technology to enhance the learning experience through videos, DVDs, computer software, and Web sites.

Use of Color: Allow students to use highlighters, sticky notes, colorful folders, and binders to organize their work.

Word Wall: Create a word wall in your classroom that lists common terminology students need to learn and apply appropriately. Be sure to incorporate color, pictures, and textures wherever possible.

Evaluating Progress: In addition to traditional assessment, student portfolios can be used to evaluate student progress and become part of the permanent observation documentation of students' performance.

Constructing Assessments: When constructing assessments, use a variety of questions including multiple choice, fill-in-the-blank, and essay. Consider creating essay questions that require discussion of only one concept at a time. For example, when asking students to identify a balanced meal, prompt them with key phrases, such as "protein, vegetable, fruit, and carbohydrate" and ask students to discuss foods from each category. Given that many students with special needs have difficulty with essay questions, allow students to list key facts and important information instead.

Assessment Accommodations: Provide students with appropriate accommodations during assessments. For example, provide extended time for students, a different assessment format, or a distraction-reduced assessment location.

Assess Essential FACS Content: As an FACS teacher, you want to test students on your content area. Students with difficulty in reading or math may need accommodations to take assessments. Examples include allowing students to take assessments orally, use calculators, or use adaptive technology as indicated in their IEPs. See *Section 3* for more information on assessments.

Grading Written Responses: For students who have difficulty with writing, allow them to focus on the main ideas of the assignment rather than on the mechanics of writing. Grade the student according to the quality of content, not on spelling and sentence structure.

Alternative Format: Some students with learning disabilities need print material in an alternative format (e.g., books, recipes, or tests on tape or in an electronic format). The special education teacher in your school district will work with you to convert course materials to an alternative format for those students who require this accommodation.

It takes considerable time to convert materials into an alternative format. Planning ahead is important to meeting the special needs of students with learning disabilities who require alternative formats.

Study Aids: Provide study questions, study guides, and time for questions and answers to help students review essential course content.

Students with learning disabilities may surpass their peers in some areas, while needing accommodations for reading, writing, or math tasks. Jillian's teacher recalls how Jillian excelled in her eye-hand coordination while completing a sewing project in the following case study.

Case Study

Jillian Excels with Lab Assignments

In Jillian's Life Skills class students learn about different careers and then complete a hands-on activity that relates to their career interests. We were studying careers in fashion, fabrics, clothing manufacturing, and sales. I asked students to sew on a button, one skill needed to become an alterations specialist. I provided instructions to students in multiple formats: I handed out written instructions and then verbally described the instructions as I demonstrated the technique. Students could watch, listen, or read before they tried to sew on the button. I also coached them as they did their work.

I was surprised at the wide quality range of work students turned in. Though almost all students said they hadn't sewn on buttons before, some looked much better than a first attempt. However, the sewing work that Jillian turned in was stunning! It looked like a professional had sewn on the button. Jillian said that she had never done this type of work before. She seemed somewhat matter of fact about the quality of her work, but pleased when I complimented her on it. Throughout the next few weeks, Jillian consistently turned in high quality activity work.

When we finished the clothing module, we moved to more pencil and paper activities. I was shocked at the first written paper that Jillian submitted. I had no idea what she had written. Her words bore no resemblance to the correct answers. When I asked her about it, she told me she was dyslexic. Since Jillian excelled with hands-on activities, I had no idea she had a disability.

After meeting with the special education teacher and seeing Julian's IEP, I began to test Jillian's understanding of the material through a verbal interview instead of a written assessment. With this accommodation, Jillian excelled in the Life Skills class.

Following Up Jillian's teacher learned a valuable lesson about working with students with disabilities. Jillian appeared to learn best through kinesthetic learning experiences; however, with the appropriate accommodations Jillian was able to demonstrate her competency with the course content.

Attention Deficit Hyperactivity Disorder (ADHD)

Students with ADHD or ADD (without hyperactivity) are characterized by "persistent patterns of inattention and/or hyperactivity-impulsivity that is more frequent and severe than is typically observed in individuals at a comparable level of development," according to the American Psychiatric Association, Diagnostic and Statistical Manual.

ADHD is a commonly diagnosed behavioral disorder affecting approximately five percent of school-aged children, or well over two million children. A number of conditions coexist with ADHD, such as depression, anxiety disorders, bipolar and conduct disorders, or oppositional defiant disorder. The percentage of students with ADHD who are also identified as having a learning disability ranges from 25–50 percent.

Students with ADHD who are not being treated with either medication or a behavior management program are frequently and easily distracted by sounds, activities, and other non-essential information. These students may have difficulty with relationships, fail in school, and experience low self-esteem if they are not treated for ADHD. Although IDEA, the federal law guiding special education services, does not recognize ADHD as a disability category, students with ADHD can be served under the "other health impairments" category and receive special education services.

ADHD Challenges

Students with ADHD may have difficulty with one or more of the following areas:

- ◆ Concentration.
- ◆ Following directions.
- ◆ Distractibility.
- ◆ Listening.
- ◆ Organization.
- ◆ Sitting for lengthy periods.
- ◆ Completing task.
- ◆ Transitioning.
- ◆ Sedentary tasks like reading.
- ◆ Planning.

Some students with ADHD take medication for this condition. The medication may be a stimulant, which actually calms the student and helps him or her focus on tasks. Antidepressants may also be used. These medications always require a physician's prescription. Any prescriptions for students are generally kept in locked storage and dispensed at the appropriate times by the school nurse or appropriate professional. Teachers do not need to monitor whether students take their medications; however, they are often asked to complete surveys or teacher-rated behavior scales to determine the degree to which the student is engaged in various class activities.

Teaching Suggestions and Common Accommodations for Students with ADHD

In addition to the previous teaching suggestions for students with learning disabilities and those provided in *Section 2: Meeting the Needs of All Learners*, consider the following suggestions.

Assistance with Structure: Provide a course outline with clearly delineated expectations and due dates. Study guides, review sheets, and frequent opportunities for feedback are helpful in providing structure and organization.

Assessment Accommodations: Assist students in arranging for appropriate assessment accommodations with the special education specialist. Many students with ADHD use exam accommodations including extended time and distraction-reduced assessment locations.

Assistive Technology: Software programs are available that highlight text on the computer screen or actually read the text to students. Many students with ADHD have found that these programs help them focus.

Accommodate the Need for Movement: Allow students to expend energy in positive, but non-disruptive, ways. For example, some students like to doodle while others prefer to massage a stress ball or a pencil grip. Build movement into the class structure that allows students to stretch and move around the room.

Access to Class Notes: Some students have difficulty focusing and taking class notes. They need your assistance to ensure that they gain quality notes. Many teachers ask a student with good note-taking skills to share his or her notes with a student who has difficulty taking complete notes.

Classroom Distractions: If a student appears extremely distracted, it may be appropriate to encourage the student to sit near the front of the class, away from doors, air conditioning units, windows, or any other possible sources of distraction.

In the case study on page 40, notice how Chris used assistive technology (AT) to complete his Internet assignments. Assistive technology can eliminate distractions and help a student with outlining key content and organizing his or her notes.

Serious Emotional Disturbance

According to the U.S. Department of Education in 2003, currently there are approximately eight percent of students with disabilities identified as Seriously Emotionally Disturbed (SED). Students with SED may be described as emotionally disturbed, severely behaviorally handicapped, emotional and behavioral disordered, socially maladjusted, psychologically disordered, emotionally handicapped, or even psychotic if their behaviors are extremely abnormal or bizarre.

IDEA defines the term SED as, "a condition exhibiting one or more of the following characteristics over a long period of time and to a marked degree that adversely affects educational performance." These characteristics include:

- ◆ An inability to learn which cannot be explained by intellectual, sensory, and health factors.
- ◆ An inability to build or maintain satisfactory interpersonal relationships with peers and teachers.
- ◆ Inappropriate types of behavior or feelings under normal circumstances.
- ◆ A general pervasive mood of unhappiness or depression.
- ◆ A tendency to develop physical symptoms or fears associated with personal or school problems.

SED includes schizophrenia; however, it does not apply to children who are socially maladjusted, unless it is determined that they have an emotional disturbance according to IDEA.

SED Behaviors

Students with emotional and behavior disorders exhibit behavior that can be categorized as either acting out or withdrawn. Acting out behaviors include such antisocial actions as getting out of a seat, yelling, talking out, disturbing peers, hitting, fighting, complaining, or stealing. Students who are withdrawn often act immature and often do not have the social skills to make friends.

Students with psychiatric disabilities are sometimes categorized as either SED or "Other Health Impaired." Descriptions of certain types of psychiatric disorders follow:

- ◆ **Depression** is a major disorder that can begin at any age. Major depression may be characterized by a depressed mood most of each day, a lack of pleasure in most activities, insomnia, feelings of worthlessness or guilt, and/or thoughts of suicide.
- ◆ **Bipolar disorder (manic depressive disorder)** causes a person to experience periods of mania and depression. In the manic phase, a person might experience inflated self-esteem and a decreased need to sleep; however, in the depressive phase, a person may experience a lack of energy and less self-esteem and interest in family, friends, and school.
- ◆ **Anxiety disorders** can disrupt a person's ability to concentrate and cause hyperventilation, a racing heart, chest pains, dizziness, panic, and extreme fear. Examples of anxiety disorders include panic disorders, simple phobias such as agoraphobia (irrational anxiety about being in places from which escape might be difficult), and Obsessive-Compulsive Disorder (OCD).
- ◆ **Schizophrenia** can cause a person to experience delusions and hallucinations in addition to a depressed mood and flat emotional reactions.

In most situations, you will not be aware that you have a student with a psychiatric disability in your classroom. Some do not need or request any accommodations, and some require a variety of accommodations. Even though students may not show any outward signs of their disabilities, their disabilities can still be disabling. For some the disability is temporary, while for others it is chronic. With medication and/or therapy, people with emotional or psychiatric disabilities may learn to manage their symptoms.

Case Study

Assistive Technology to the Rescue

Ms. Kim requires her students to find and report on information found on the Internet. She noticed that Chris was never successful in completing the assignment during the allotted time period. She moved Chris' computer station to the one closest to the front of the room—the station with the assistive technology (AT) programs installed. She showed Chris how to use the AT so that as he was reading the words were highlighted on the screen. He also could turn the voice-recognition feature on if he didn't know all the words. Chris could adjust the speed of the voice reading as well as the tone and gender of the voice. With the AT, Chris could complete his assignments within the class period. The AT provided the support Chris needed to be successful.

Following Up With the appropriate accommodations, Chris was able to complete assignments at the same time as the remainder of his class. In what ways might assistive technology help your students?

Teaching Suggestions and Common Accommodations for Students with SED

Students with emotional disturbances and/or psychiatric disabilities need a nurturing and safe classroom environment.

Supportive Environment: Many students with psychiatric disabilities fear stigmatization because of their disability. If a student shares with you about his or her disability, be supportive and welcoming when a student requests assistance in arranging for accommodations, such as extended time on assessments.

Clearly Defined Learning Goals: A course outline with clearly delineated statements about your expectations is helpful to students who need help with structure and organization. The course outline and learning goals can serve as an "advanced organizer" to prepare the student for upcoming assignments and assessments.

Assessment Accommodations: Upon request, assist students in arranging for assessment accommodations, such as extra time or a distraction-reduced assessment location.

Make-up Work: Collaborate with students about arrangements to make up tests and other assignments, allowing them extra time since these students may miss school due to serious psychiatric episodes.

Web-enhanced Learning: If classroom materials are available on the Web, students with emotional or psychiatric disabilities may be able to engage in learning via the Internet. Learning through computer access is becoming a popular medium for students whose disabilities prevent them from participating in traditional classroom activities.

Inappropriate Behavior: Students with disabilities are subject to the same code of conduct required of any student at your school. If there are incidences of inappropriate behavior, give concise and honest feedback about behaviors that are inappropriate. If there are situations involving threats or abusive behavior, always follow your school policy.

Gifted and Talented Students

The Gifted and Talented Children's Act defines students who are gifted and talented as those, "possessing demonstrated or potential abilities that give evidence of high performance capability in such areas as intellectual, creative, specific academic or leadership ability, or in the performing or visual arts, and who by reason thereof require services or activities not ordinarily provided by the school."

Students who are gifted and talented need specialized educational programs in the form of modified curriculum and specialized instructional activities to enhance their individual talents. These students may likely become our outstanding leaders, scientists, artists, researchers, and inventors.

Students with learning, sensory, or physical disabilities may also be gifted and talented students. Through the IDEA law, these students are eligible for special education services, including accommodations and supports as determined through the IEP process. In order for gifted and talented students with disabilities to reach their potential, it is critical that their intellectual strengths be recognized and nurtured. At the same time, their disabilities should be appropriately accommodated.

Gifted and Talented Traits

Gifted students with disabilities often use their intellectual gifts to try to circumvent their disabilities. According to the ERIC Clearinghouse on *Disabilities and Gifted Education*, students who are gifted and talented:

- Are often perfectionistic and idealistic. They may equate self-esteem and self-worth with achievement and grades.
- May be at different developmental levels at the same time regarding their chronological ages and physical, social, emotional, and intellectual development.
- Are learners who rapidly acquire, retain, and use large amounts of information.
- Are highly sensitive to criticism, yet may appear careless, as evidenced by losing their assignments, forgetting their homework, or being disorganized.

- Are often bored, as evidenced by poor attention, daydreaming, and low tolerance for persistence on tasks that they don't see as relevant to themselves.
- Are problem solvers who often reframe questions and create novel solutions to problems.

Teaching Suggestions and Common Accommodations for Students Who Are Gifted and Talented

Students who are gifted and talented need to be exposed to challenging and conceptually rich curricula. School districts have typically implemented four strategies to address the needs of these students:

- **Acceleration:** Provides opportunities for the student to move through the required content at a faster pace. For example, students may skip a grade, test out of courses, and/or be placed in a more challenging math class while remaining in regular classes for other content areas.
- **Curriculum Compacting:** Involves compressing the instructional content and materials so that academically able students have more time to work on challenging projects.
- **Enrichment:** Involves adding new and different information from a variety of disciplines outside the traditional curriculum.
- **Curriculum Outside the Classroom:** Involves the use of mentors, internships, and special projects to enhance learning experiences. Using community resources to supplement the education of students who are gifted and talented is commonly implemented to meet the special needs of this population.

Specific strategies that you can implement to maximize the time that students who are gifted and talented spend in your classroom follow.

Engage Students in Independent Inquiry: Allow students an opportunity to negotiate self-directed research projects that meet and expand your course objectives.

Relevant Learning Environment: Implement a flexibly structured learning environment that converts your classroom into a laboratory that closely resembles the real world.

Instructional Considerations: Provide individual pacing and challenging activities at an advanced level. Promote self-direction that enables students to use their strengths and preferred learning styles.

Mentoring Programs: The opportunity to work with mentors who demonstrate how classroom learning objectives are implemented in real-world settings is a powerful learning experience for students.

Classroom Dynamics: Discuss the implications of your students' capabilities and special learning needs. If classroom questions arise regarding special needs, deal with them openly and honestly; however, these types of questions and answers should be discussed on an individual basis. Expect participation in all activities and treat each student with respect. Celebrate individual differences.

Summary

Remember, it's your responsibility to support your school's commitment to equal access to education. This information will help you deliver a quality education to all students, including students who are gifted and talented as well as to students with disabilities. Contact a special education teacher if you have questions or concerns about the students in your classroom.

Section 5: Teaching Students with Sensory, Orthopedic, and Other Health Impairments

Students with sensory or orthopedic impairments, such as those who are visually, hearing, or mobility impaired are being educated in the inclusive classroom with more and more frequency. As an FACS teacher, you will have the challenge of teaching independent living skills to your classes. Students that have these types of impairments may need the input or assistance of an occupational, physical, or speech therapist to achieve certain goals. Therapists and teachers working together make a successful team.

Visual Impairments (VI)

IDEA defines a visual impairment as, "impairment in vision that, even with correction, adversely affects a child's educational performance." Students who are blind or visually impaired vary considerably. For example, some have no vision; others are able to see large forms; others can see print if magnified; and still others have tunnel vision with no peripheral vision or the reverse. Recent IDEA statistics indicate that there are more than 290,000 students with visual impairments.

Students with visual impairments are classified according to their use of vision and/or tactile means for learning as follows:

- **Totally Blind:** A student who receives no useful information through the sense of vision and relies on hearing and tactile information for learning.
- **Functionally Blind:** A student who has so little vision that he or she learns primarily through the other senses. Students who are blind or functionally blind typically use braille to read and write.
- **Low Vision:** Students with low vision comprise between 75–80 percent of the school-age visually impaired population. These students have enough vision to read print, often with the assistance of technology that enlarges the print size.

Quick Facts

Technology for the Blind and Visually Impaired

Educational access for the blind and visually impaired is greatly enhanced through advances in computer technology including hardware and software. Type magnification, talking word processors, screen-reader software, braille translation software, and braille embossers and keyboards are just a few of the augmentative aids available.

Students with sensory impairments, such as those who are blind, visually impaired, deaf, or hearing impaired often bring auxiliary aids and adaptive equipment to the classroom. For example, Joshua has a white cane to help him navigate around the school. While he is able to use braille, he uses technology, such as a Type-N-Speak™ apparatus, to take notes during class. Joshua, like many students with disabilities, knows what accommodations he needs. The best strategy for the classroom teacher is to relax and get to know Joshua. Meet with Joshua and the school's special education staff to seek out what support services are necessary to meet his needs.

As you work with students like Joshua, or other students with hearing, orthopedic, or other health impairments, you'll find the support you need from the special education teachers, and/or the Individualized Education Program (IEP) team members. Ask to be included on the IEP team to discuss what goals and objectives are appropriate for Joshua to learn. Also ask what supports and accommodations are recommended to assist Joshua with meeting his goals. As an educator, you are responsible for considering the needs of every student when teaching. Your instruction—whether it includes lectures, Web sites, videos, overheads, handouts, and textbooks—must be accessible to all students.

See how Joshua accomplished his goals in the case study on page 44.

CASE STUDY

Joshua Cooks with Tape-Recorded Recipes

Because Joshua could not read visually, the vision specialist suggested using tape-recorded or braille recipes. A special apron was made with two extra pockets: one to hold the tape recorder near Joshua's waist, and a second pocket to hold an on/off switch so he could turn off the recorder to follow the directions before hearing the next step. Joshua and his classroom teacher, Mrs. Moffet, selected an "easy-to-prepare" dish that all her students learned to cook: macaroni and cheese. The vision specialist recorded the recipe on tape for Joshua and had a braille version prepared just in case he preferred it.

Joshua worked with another student who was also learning the same recipe and who could help Joshua navigate the kitchen supplies and appliances. Before they began cooking, Mrs. Moffet gave Joshua some mobility and orientation strategies of the room. She then gave him a tactile overview of the range. Joshua could feel the dials and the burners, and became familiar with which dial turned on which burner. Joshua learned how to set the burner to warm by counting the clicks of the dial. As Mrs. Moffet guided Joshua's hand while turning the dial, she said, "1...2...3 clicks and you're on a low-medium setting."

As Joshua read each step of the recipe, he would tell his team member the step and together they would follow the directions. Mrs. Moffet watched closely each time the students were cooking on the range to assure that there were no accidents. Mrs. Moffet encouraged Joshua to listen carefully for a bubbling sound. A slow simmer has a gentle bubbling sound. This would help Joshua avoid boil overs and prepare the macaroni and cheese according to recipe directions.

Following Up You can see how successful that Joshua must have felt. This team approach not only provided an entrée to share, it developed a friendship between Joshua and his lab partner.

Teaching Strategies and Accommodations for Students with Visual Impairments

Students who have low vision or are blind are constantly challenged by classroom instructional strategies. Although they can easily hear lectures and discussions, it can be difficult for them to access class notes. Textbooks, overhead transparencies, PowerPoint® presentations, maps, videos, written exams, demonstrations, library materials, and videos present their challenges for the visually impaired. In many classrooms, a large part of traditional learning is visual. Fortunately, many students with visual disabilities have developed other strategies to learn.

Some students with visual impairments use braille, and some have little or no knowledge of braille. They may use a variety of equipment, accommodations, and compensatory strategies based upon their widely varying needs. Many make use of assistive technology (AT), especially print-to-voice conversion using a scanner and voice production software. Textbooks are often converted and put on disks for later use. Others use taped textbooks and equipment to enlarge the type (such as closed circuit television [CCTV]), or actual print enlargements. Other common accommodations for students with visual impairments are described as follows. For some additional tips for working with students with visual impairments, see Figure 5-1.

Orientation to Classroom: You should set up some time for the student to explore the physical layout of the room with locations of steps, furniture, lecture position, low-hanging objects, or any other obstacles. It's especially important to allow the student to tactilely familiarize him- or herself with any appliances or equipment prior to using it.

White Canes: People who are blind or visually impaired may use white canes for mobility and orientation. They must receive training to use a cane effectively.

Preferential Seating: Students with visual impairments may need preferential seating since they depend heavily upon listening. These students may want the same anonymity as other students, so it is important that you avoid pointing out the student or the alternative arrangements to others in the class.

Use of Language: Although it is unnecessary to rewrite the entire course, you can help a student with a visual impairment by avoiding phrases such as, "Look at this." Use descriptive language instead. Repeat aloud what is written on an overhead or the board.

Arranging for Accommodations: A meeting with the student is essential to facilitate the arrangement of accommodations and auxiliary aids which may include, in addition to assessment accommodations, access to class notes and/or the taping of lectures; print material in alternative format; a script with verbal descriptions of videos or slides, charts, and graphs, or other such visual depictions converted to tactile representations.

Lab Assistance: These students may need a lab partner during hands-on activities. Assist the student in finding a partner. In some cases, a teacher aide may accompany the student to class for special assistance. Introduce yourself to the teacher aide and provide an overview of the lesson.

Print Material in Alternative Format: For students who will require class materials in alternative formats, have copies of the course outline and reading assignments ready three to five weeks prior to planned use. The vision specialist will convert these materials into braille, enlarged print, audiotapes, or another alternative format. Conversion of materials takes time. It is important that students with visual impairments have access to class materials at the same time as others in your class. Coordinate alternative formats with your district's special education teachers.

Assessment Accommodations: Assessment accommodations, which may include assistive technology, a reader/scribe and extra time, a computer, closed circuit TV (CCTV), braille, enlargements, tapes, and/or image enhanced materials, may be needed. Coordinate these arrangements with special education teachers or vision specialist.

Figure 5-1

Tips for Working with Students with Visual Impairments
• Allow the vision specialist or special education teacher adequate time to prepare braille, photo enlargements, and/or taped materials for a visually impaired student. This may mean planning what assignments and/or materials you will use more in advance of a given lesson.
• Obtain permission to tape classroom discussions following your school policy.
• Orally describe procedures during all demonstrations. You may also want to create written descriptions of demonstration procedures for translation into braille or other media.
• Report any misuse of any specialized equipment or auxiliary aids on the part of the student.
• Allow the student ample time to explore new and unfamiliar classroom and school environments.
• Allow the student additional time to complete assignments when his or her reading medium is assistive technology (AT), braille, large print, or audiotapes.
• Encourage the student to wear or use any prescriptive lenses or other low vision aids.
• Allow students to hold printed materials close to the eyes. It will not harm their eyes.
• Older students who have reached a level of self-acceptance may be willing to share information about their visual impairment with their classmates. Encourage this whenever possible.

Hearing Impairments (HI)

IDEA uses the term "hearing impairments" to indicate the types of hearing loss for which special education and related services are needed, such as those who are deaf or hard-of-hearing.

- **Deaf:** Someone who is "deaf" is not able to use hearing to understand speech, even with hearing aids.
- **Hard-of-Hearing:** A person who is "hard-of-hearing" has a significant hearing loss that makes some special adaptations necessary. Hard-of-hearing students can hear some speech with hearing aids and become familiar with common teaching strategies and accommodations.

Students who are deaf or hard-of-hearing do not all have the same characteristics.

- Some have a measure of usable residual hearing and use a device to amplify sounds (an FM system).
- Some choose to speak while others use very little or no oral communication.
- Some students are extremely adept at speech reading, while others have very limited ability to "read lips."
- Some students prefer American Sign Language (ASL)—a visual-gestural language with its own rules of syntax, semantics, and symbols—and/or finger spelling—a process of spelling each letter of a word to communicate.

In the following case study, Mrs. McHugh realizes the importance of an interpreter.

Case Study

Peers Learn Signing to Talk with Bill

As she went over her fall class list, Mrs. McHugh noticed that a student with a hearing impairment enrolled in her foods class. Bill would attend the class with his interpreter. Mrs. McHugh wondered how having the interpreter present would impact her class.

Mrs. McHugh found that having the interpreter, Mr. Lewis, in her class did not give her an extra pair of hands and eyes. Instead, he followed Bill and interpreted as Bill talked with his classmates.

Mrs. McHugh realized that Mr. Lewis was doing something much more important than just helping Bill out. Bill's classmates were very interested in knowing more about American Sign Language (ASL), the sign language that Bill and his interpreter used to communicate. The class kept asking Mr. Lewis how to sign. Mr. Lewis taught the class some basic communication signs that they used to talk with Bill. Mrs. McHugh saw Bill interacting more and more directly with his peers as their "sign vocabulary" grew. She noticed during her assigned lunch duty that Bill had made several friends and that they were eating lunch together and signing without the assistance of Mr. Lewis. All of the students, and even the teachers, learned an important lesson about the benefits of inclusion by having Bill and his interpreter in the classroom. Mrs. McHugh said, "Not only are my students getting the satisfaction of learning ASL and talking with Bill, but they also are learning compassion and respect for others."

Following Up Mr. Lewis successfully helped Bill accomplish his communication needs. Everyone in the class enhanced their communication skills by interacting with Bill and Mr. Lewis. See Figure 5-2 on page 48 for more information about using an interpreter.

Quick Facts

Cochlear Implants

Since cochlear implants destroy residual hearing, their use is limited to those people who are totally deaf. For students who are hard-of-hearing, choose one or more forms of assistive technology to enhance learning.

Teaching Strategies and Accommodations for Students with Hearing Impairments

Individuals who are hearing impaired rely upon visual input rather than auditory input when communicating. Using visual aspects of communication (e.g., body language, gestures, and facial expression) often feels awkward to people who are accustomed to the auditory world. However, you can learn to effectively communicate with students who are deaf or hard-of-hearing. Review the suggestions that follow to become familiar with common teaching strategies and accommodations.

Gaining Attention: Make sure that you have a deaf student's attention before speaking to him or her. A light touch on the shoulder, a wave, or other visual signal will help.

Preferential Seating: Offer the student preferential seating near the front of the classroom so that he or she can clearly see a sign language interpreter and get as much from visual and auditory clues as possible.

Effective Communication: Don't talk with your back to the class when writing on the board. It eliminates any chance of the student getting facial or speech reading cues. Your face and mouth need to be clearly visible at all times.

Videos and Slides: Provide videos and slides with captioning. If captioning is not available, supply an outline or summary of the materials covered. If an interpreter is in the classroom, make sure that he or she is visible to the special needs student.

Class Discussion: When students make comments in class or ask questions, repeat the questions before answering, or phrase your answers in such a way that the questions are obvious.

Class Notes: Students may need your assistance in getting class notes. When a student is using a sign language interpreter, captioning, or lip-reading, it is difficult to take good notes.

Real-time Captioning Services: When a student uses real-time captioning services, a professional sits in the class and types the lecture/conversation onto a screen that the student reads.

Sign-Language Services: When a student uses a sign language interpreter, discuss with both the student and interpreter where the interpreter should be located to provide the greatest benefit for the student without distracting other class members.

Role of the Interpreter: The interpreter is in the classroom only to facilitate communication. He or she should not be asked to run errands, proctor exams, or discuss the student's personal issues. He or she should not participate in the class in any way.

Interpreter Classroom Etiquette: The interpreter is in the classroom to facilitate communication for both the student and the instructor. Speak directly to the student, even though it may be the interpreter who clarifies information for you. Likewise, the interpreter may request clarification from you to ensure accuracy of the information conveyed. See Figure 5-2 on page 48.

Augmentative Communication: Some students cannot learn to communicate by using ASL because of other physical or cognitive disabilities. These students often use Augmentative and Alternative Communication (AAC). AAC is a diverse set of nonspeech communication devices, strategies, and methods to assist the nonspeaking with the ability to communicate with others. Most augmentative communication devices use a series of symbols that the student selects to communicate. Some devices use synthetic speech to "talk" as the student selects a symbol. Many of these devices will be programmed with a working vocabulary that the student uses to communicate with teachers and peers. When communicating with a student who uses an AAC device, find out how the communication system works. Be patient while the student constructs a message. It takes longer than conventional speech. Interact with the student at eye level. If the student uses a wheelchair, you might sit across from him or her. Talk directly to the student. Don't be afraid to say you don't understand something and to ask to have it repeated. Be sure you give the student an opportunity to ask questions or to make a comment. Remember, communication is a two-way process.

English Language Learners: For many deaf students, English is a second language. When grading written assignments and/or essay tests, look for accurate and comprehensive content rather than writing style.

Figure 5-2

While Using Interpreting Services
• **Speak Directly to the Student.** Because the interpreter is in the classroom to facilitate communication for both the student and instructor, speak directly to and maintain communication with the student. The interpreter may request clarification from you and/or the student to ensure accuracy of the information conveyed.
• **Spell Out Technical Words.** It is helpful to have technical terms or jargon relating to a particular discipline or concept spelled or written out, either on the board, an overhead projector, a class handout, or some other visual aid.
• **Speak at a Reasonable Pace.** Interpreters normally interpret with a time lag of one or two sentences after the speaker because interpreters must first process the information before relaying it. Speak naturally at a modest pace, keeping in mind that the interpreter must listen and understand a complete thought before signing it.
• **Use "I" and "You" References.** The interpreter will relay your exact words. Use personal references such as "I" and "You" when communicating with individuals who are deaf or hard-of-hearing. Avoid speaking of the individual in the third person; phrases such as "ask her" or "tell him" can be confusing.
• **Encourage Communicating in Turn.** It is important that only one person speaks or signs at a time. The interpreting process only allows one person to communicate at a time. Therefore, encourage students to wait before speaking or signing until you acknowledge them.
• **Allow Ample Time for Reading.** The student cannot read and watch the interpreter at the same time. Avoid talking while students are focused on written work or overhead multimedia presentations. Allow enough time for the student to read all the materials.
• **Recognize the Need for a Note-taker.** It is difficult to take good notes while lip reading or watching a sign language interpreter. Therefore, a note-taker may be both a helpful and reasonable accommodation in these instances.
• **Allow Ample Time for Questions.** During class discussions or question/answer periods, give the student an opportunity to raise his or her hand, be recognized, and ask questions through the interpreter. Making time for questions allows the interpreter to finish interpreting for the current speaker and enables the student who is deaf or hard-of-hearing to participate in class.
• **Repeat or Paraphrase Questions and Responses.** When questions are asked, be sure to repeat or paraphrase questions before giving a response. Likewise, repeat or paraphrase responses.
• **Incorporate Strategic Lecture Breaks.** Plan periodic breaks so that both student and interpreter can rest from the rigors of interpreting.

Orthopedic Impairments

Students with orthopedic impairments may have difficulty with mobility and coordination. Orthopedic impairments can involve all or part of a person's skeletal system including limbs, muscles, joints, and bones.

According to the IDEA law, orthopedic impairments must be severe and adversely affect a student's educational performance. Orthopedic impairments may be caused by:

- Congenital anomaly, such as a club foot or missing limb.
- Diseases, such as polio or bone tuberculosis.
- Conditions such as cerebral palsy, amputations, musular dystrophy, or spinal cord injury.

While some students may be ambulatory, others may use crutches, braces, walkers, or wheelchairs. See Figure 5-3 on page 49.

Figure 5-3

Characteristics of Physical Impairments	
Orthopedic	Involves deformities of the skeletal system—bones, joints, limbs, and associated muscles.
Neurological	Involves the nervous system—affecting the ability to move, use, feel, or control certain parts of the body.
Monoplegia	Involves partial or total paralysis of one limb (arm or leg).
Hemiplegia	Involves partial or total paralysis of one side of the body.
Triplegia	Involves partial or total paralysis of three limbs.
Paraplegia	Involves varying degrees of paralysis of the lower half of the body including both legs.
Quadriplegia	Paralysis of both arms and legs. Movement of trunk and face may also be affected.
Spina Bifida (Mylodysplasia)	A congenital neural tube defect in which the spine fails to close properly during the early months of pregnancy leaving a lesion in the spine. This lesion in the vertebrae may damage the nerves that control muscles and feelings in the lower part of the body. Partial or total paralysis may occur at the point of the lesion or below.
Cerebral Palsy (CP)	A disorder of voluntary movement and posture that may include paralysis, extreme weakness, lack of coordination, involuntary convulsions, and other motor disorders resulting from damage to the brain before, during, or shortly after birth.
Muscular Dystrophy (MD)	A group of progressive genetic diseases that attack and weaken the body's muscles. Often times by age 10 to 14, students with muscular dystrophy lose the ability to walk due to the atrophy or degeneration of the leg muscles.
Spinal Cord Injury	An injury to the spine most often caused by an auto or sports accident resulting in impairments to body parts and organs below the spinal injury.

Other Health Impairments

Other health impairments are often less visible. According to IDEA, these impairments cause limited strength, vitality, or alertness that result in limited alertness in the educational environment. They can be caused by such conditions as arthritis, asthma, cancer, sickle cell anemia, attention deficit disorder or attention deficit hyperactivity disorder, orthopedic limitations, post surgery, chronic fatigue syndrome, or seizure disorder. The student may have limited energy; difficulty walking, standing, or sitting for a long time; or other disabling characteristics, such as an inability to write or control body movements.

Functional limitations may be episodic for some students who may experience dizziness, disorientation, and difficulty breathing during an occurrence. For example, with asthma or a seizure disorder, a student may have periods when he or she functions without any accommodations, but at other times functional limitations are quite severe, such as possible incontinence during a seizure. See Figure 5-4 on page 50.

Figure 5-4

Characteristics of Other Health Impairments	
Asthma	A chronic lung disease characterized by episodic bouts of wheezing, coughing, and difficulty breathing. An asthmatic attack can be triggered by allergens (e.g., pollen, pets, and foods), irritants (e.g., smoke, smog), emotional stress, or exercise.
Diabetes	A chronic disorder of carbohydrate metabolism by which a person's body is not able to produce or properly use insulin (a hormone produced by the pancreas) to convert sugars, starches, and other foods for adequate energy. Early symptoms include thirst, headaches, weight loss, frequent urination, and wounds that are slow to heal.
Epilepsy	A neurological seizure disorder marked by sudden, disturbed electrical rhythms of the central nervous system that may include involuntary transient impairment of consciousness, sensation, memory. Most students with epilepsy have normal intelligence.
Cystic Fibrosis	A genetic disorder in which the body's exocrine glands excrete thick mucus that can block the lungs and parts of the digestive system. This can result in difficulty breathing and loss of excessive salt in sweat.

Teaching Strategies and Accommodations for Students with Orthopedic Impairments and Other Health Impairments

Even with the same disability, students with mobility or medical impairments may have a wide variety of characteristics. For example, people who have experienced a spinal cord injury are likely to show differing degrees of limitation. They may require different types of classroom accommodations or may need no accommodations.

Showing Compassion: Some students with orthopedic or other health impairments lose control over certain body parts or functions. For example, students with some types of cerebral palsy (CP) often have involuntary muscle spasms. When a student with CP tries to pick up a pencil, his or her arm may wave wildly. A student with epilepsy may have a seizure in which his or her body may shake violently. He or she may fall from a sitting or standing position, may drool, or may have incontinence. Teach other students to ignore these behaviors and show compassion.

Assessment Accommodations: Students who have upper body limitations and who are unable to use their hands will likely need accommodations, such as extended time, a scribe, or voice recognition software. Assist the student in coordinating these accommodations with the special educator in your school.

Access to Class Notes: Students who are unable to use their hands may need assistance in finding a note taker, or they may elect to tape record lectures.

Classroom Aides: Some students have a classroom aide who accompanies them to the FACS classroom and assists them with taking notes, completing class assignments, and dealing with mobility issues. Review the interpreter guidelines in Figure 5-2 for additional tips in working with classroom aides.

Tardiness: Some students are unable to quickly get from one location to another due to difficulty in using adaptive transportation. For these reasons, a student may be late getting to class. Please be patient when this happens; it is not usually done by choice.

Seating Arrangements: In a few situations, a student may be unable to use the type of chair provided in the classroom. The special education teacher will assist you and the student in making special seating arrangements, when necessary.

Inaccessible Classroom: If your classroom's equipment is inaccessible to a student, discuss several strategies for making your classroom accessible with the principal and special educator in your building. For example, perhaps one work station could be equipped with a lower table to accommodate a wheelchair.

Laboratory Courses: Some students may need assistance for laboratory courses. These students may need to be paired with an able-bodied student or a teaching assistant. Consult a special educator if you need assistance in making these arrangements.

Missed Classes: Some students experience recurrence of a chronic condition requiring bed rest and/or hospitalization. These students need extra time to complete work and the opportunity to make up assessments. Other arrangements may be necessary if a student misses class excessively.

Field Trips: Make arrangements for barrier-free field trips so that all students are able to experience out of school activities. Some accommodations that you may need to arrange may be bus transportation that has an accessible entrance for boarding and/or a wheelchair lift. Make sure that the field trip destination is barrier-free.

Physical, Occupational, and/or Speech Therapy: Each school district must provide physical, occupational, and speech therapy for students who need these services.

- A physical therapist is a professional who helps people with disabilities develop and maintain muscular and orthopedic capabilities through instruction with stretching, positioning, or adjusting of mobility equipment.
- An occupational therapist is a professional who programs or delivers instructional activities, materials, or adaptive equipment to assist with fine-motor activities and activities of daily living.
- A speech therapist is a professional who deals with communication problems involving articulation, language, fluency, voice, and augmentative communication needs.

General Considerations for Teaching All Students with Disabilities

Students with orthopedic, mobility, or other health impairments want to have a positive school experience like other students. They want to have friends and experience the benefits of an education. You, as the FACS teacher, have an important role in facilitating a classroom environment that models acceptance, while challenging all students to exceed beyond their own expectations. The following suggestions are provided to assist you in challenging all students to perform their best.

Universal Design for Learning: As stated in *Section 2*, universal design is an approach to designing course instruction, materials, and content to benefit people of all learning styles without adaptation or retrofitting. By incorporating universal design principles in instruction that allow students with disabilities access to the classroom, you may also be designing instruction that works better for everyone in the class.

Guided Notes: Providing students with guided notes helps them focus on appropriate material and enables them to learn more effectively. Some students with disabilities have difficulty taking notes. They may need assistance in getting a volunteer note-taker, or a copy of class notes, and/or copies of overheads and other class materials.

Expectations: Although many students with disabilities need accommodations, expect these students to perform at a level equal to their abilities. Assessment and evaluation activities need to meet the criteria outlined in the IEP.

Collaboration: Don't hesitate to call parents or special educators to arrange for a meeting to discuss school-related issues.

Inappropriate Behavior: Students with disabilities are subject to the same code of conduct required of any student in your district. Give concise and honest feedback about behaviors that are inappropriate.

Summary

Teaching students with sensory, orthopedic, or other health impairments offers its own set of challenges. Developing creative options to help these students succeed can involve many IEP team members as well as the students in the FACS classroom. Working together provides an opportunity to learn compassion and acceptance of others.

Section 6: Teaching Students with Cognitive Impairments/Mental Retardation

Students with cognitive impairment/mental retardation may have mental and/or physical impairments that are likely to continue indefinitely. Examples include, but are not limited to, fetal alcohol syndrome or Down syndrome. According to the U.S. Department of Education, over 10 percent of the students served under IDEA have a cognitive impairment/mental retardation. *(Please note that while current legislation refers to cognitive impairment as mental retardation, discussion continues about changing this terminology.)*

What Is Cognitive Impairment/Mental Retardation?

Three criteria are required for identifying a student as cognitively impaired/mentally retarded under the IDEA definition. The student must meet all three of the following criteria:

1. Significantly below-average intelligence.
2. Significantly below-average adaptive behavior skills—or the skills needed to live, work, and play in the community.
3. A history of below-average intelligence and adaptive behaviors since childhood, defined as before age 18.

School psychologists or family doctors typically conduct both intelligence and adaptive behavior testing to see how a student performs. In some school systems, because of the stigma often attached to the term "mental retardation," other labels are used, such as cognitive impairment or developmental disability. All of these terms refer to the same thing—significantly below-average cognitive functioning.

Significantly Below-Average Intelligence. This means the student scored two or more standard deviations below the mean on a standardized intelligence test, such as the Wechsler Intelligence Scale for Children (WISC). The student's performance on the test indicates where the student is functioning in terms of age-appropriate intellectual abilities. For example, if a student's intelligence quotient (IQ) falls between 55 and 75, the student is classified as mildly mentally retarded as long as the student is less than age 18 and meets the listed adaptive behavior criteria.

Quick Facts

Levels of Cognitive Impairment/ Mental Retardation

Level	IQ Test Score
Mild	55 to 70 (to 75)
Moderate	40 to 55
Severe	25 to 40
Profound	Below 25

(Since the standard error of measurement for most IQ tests is approximately five points, the top range may go to 75. Average intelligence is considered 100.)

Significantly Below-Average Adaptive Behavior Skills. According to the American Association on Mental Retardation (AAMR), adaptive behavior skills fit into three general areas: conceptual skills, social skills, and practical living skills. These skills are measured with standardized assessments. Significantly below-average adaptive behavior skills are defined as being at least two standard deviations below average in one of the three categories of adaptive behavior or in an overall score of all three. A student must be deficient in at least one item from each category in order to qualify for services under IDEA. See Figure 6-1 on page 53.

Figure 6-1

Adaptive Behavior Skills		
Conceptual Skills	**Social Skills**	**Practical Living Skills**
• Receptive and expressive language skills. • Reading and writing skills. • Money management skills. • Self-direction.	• Interpersonal skills. • Responsibility. • Self-esteem. • Gullibility (the likelihood of being duped or manipulated by others; avoids victimization). • Following rules and obeying laws.	• Activities of daily living—eating, dressing, bathing, toileting, and mobility. • Instrumental activities of daily living—using the telephone, housekeeping chores, preparing meals, managing money, using transportation services, and handling health issues, such as taking medication. • Occupational/career skills. • Safety skills.

Conditions Must Occur in Childhood. The student must have had the conditions mentioned above since childhood, which is defined as age 18 or below. The developmental observation period before age 18 differentiates between mental retardation and an adult with impaired performance.

To be defined in IDEA under the category of mental retardation (cognitive impairment), a student must be significantly below-average in intellect, have poor adaptive behavior in three distinct areas, and have been diagnosed prior to age 18 to meet the criteria. Any student who does not meet these standards is not qualified to receive assistance under the IDEA category of mental retardation (cognitive impairment).

Brain Development and Learning Success

The brain plays a major role in learning success. According to Dr. Mel Levine, Professor of pediatrics at the University of North Carolina Medical School, author, and cofounder of a non-profit institute called *All Kinds of Minds,* students with cognitive impairments/mental retardation may have learning strengths or difficulties with any combination of the following areas of neuro-development:

1. Attention.
2. Temporal sequential ordering.
3. Spatial ordering.
4. Memory.
5. Language.
6. Neuromotor functions.
7. Social cognition.
8. Higher order cognition.

The degree of strength or difficulty in any of the eight areas listed is different for each student. How will you accommodate all the different learning strengths, challenges, and styles of your students? In order to enhance their learning experiences, you need to present information to students using as many of the five senses as possible. See Figure 6-2 on page 54.

Imagine using only one method to teach, such as lecturing. Students receive information in only an auditory manner and do not have the benefit of experiencing the content through other senses. The use of cooking demonstrations in a foods class gives students multiple opportunities to absorb learning—they can see, smell, and taste.

The FACS curriculum provides many opportunities for students with cognitive impairments/mental retardation to learn according to their personal strengths.

Once students with cognitive impairments/mental retardation finish high school, the lessons learned in your class may help them make career choices they never thought possible.

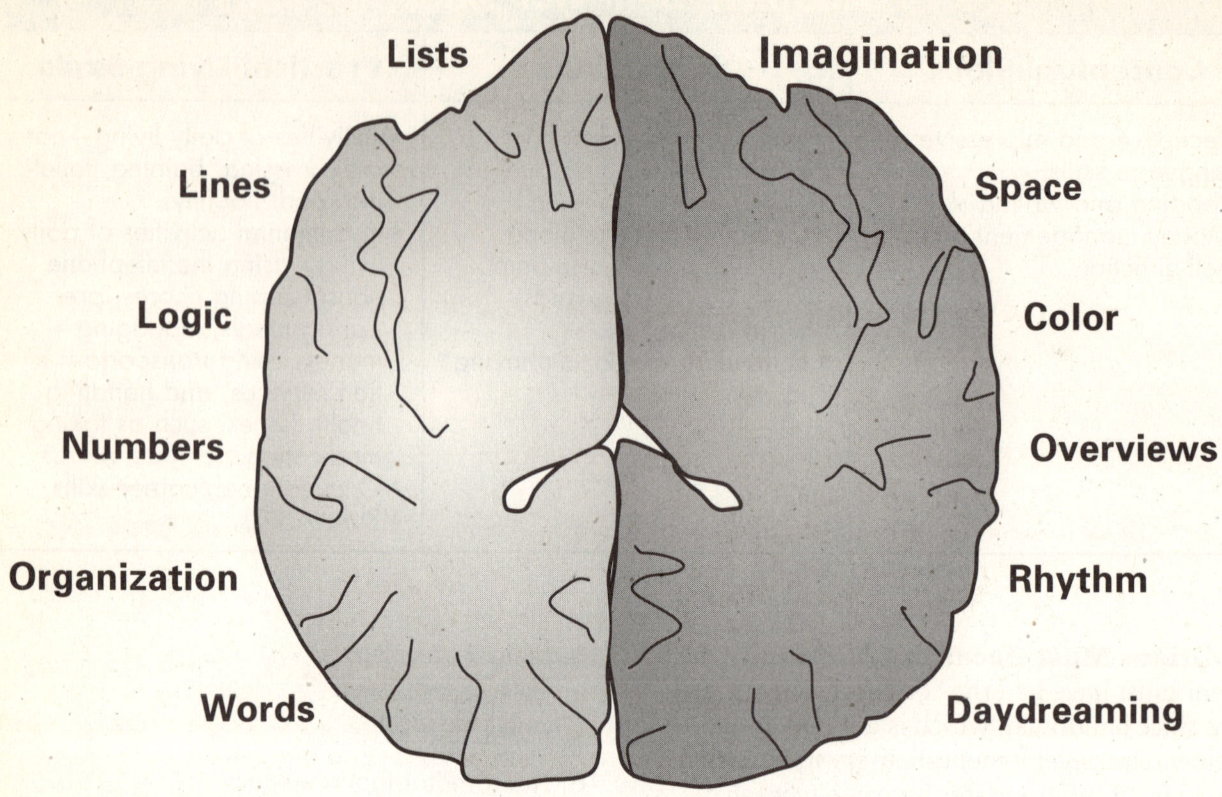

Figure 6-2 The brain is a fantastic organ. It consumes one-fifth of the oxygen you take in. Drinking water, exercising, and breathing all increase the amount of oxygen the body delivers to the brain. Scientists believe the brain has a logical left and creative right side with each half responsible for specific information. The logical left side handles lists, lines, logic, numbers, organization, and words. The creative right side works with imagination, space, color, overviews, rhythm, and daydreaming.

Causes of Cognitive Impairment/ Mental Retardation

Understanding the causes of cognitive impairment/mental retardation is both complex and challenging. The two primary causes of cognitive impairment/mental retardation involve biological or environmental factors. However, often factors from both categories are involved. For about one third of the people with cognitive impairment/mental retardation, the cause is unknown.

- **Biological** refers to a physiological source and may be a genetic disorder, cranial malformation, or poor prenatal care. The best-known and most prevalent example of a biological cause is Down syndrome, a genetic disorder.
- **Environmental** refers to a psychological or sociological cause for cognitive impairment/mental retardation and may include personality, psychiatric, developmental, family, living, or lifestyle choices. Drug abuse, alcohol abuse, and learned helplessness are also examples of psychological or sociological environmental causes. According to Ed Zigler, a prominent psychologist, the five personality features commonly observed in cognitive impairment/mental retardation related to learned helplessness include a low expectation of success, fear of failure, need for social reinforcement, outer directedness, and overdependency on others.

Teaching Strategies and Accommodations for Students with Cognitive Impairments/Mental Retardation

When you challenge students to try new things, work cooperatively, and respect their classmates, you encourage the educational process. Having students jointly develop class rules, posting the rules in a visible location, and referring to the rules as needed helps everyone take ownership of the process.

Including students with cognitive impairment/mental retardation in the classroom will give all your students an opportunity to work with others who bring strengths and challenges to the learning environment. Many adults with cognitive impairments/mental retardation hold productive jobs in supermarkets, restaurants, and other business settings. Life skills, social skills, and peer training are all areas where you can make a difference. How do you accomplish this? First, you need to develop an accepting environment.

Accepting Environment: Students in the inclusive classroom may have many questions about their fellow students. On a continuous basis, indicate you expect team and peer support. Encourage students to become positive role models for others. Remind students that ridicule or laughing will not be tolerated. Help each student experience the joy of accomplishing goals no matter how small.

Routines and Structure: Provide instructional routines and structure to make sure the learning environment is predictable. Many students with special needs have difficulty coping with change. Consistency at the beginning and ending of class can provide a structure that enables your students with special needs to know what to expect.

Teaching in Natural Environments: Teach food preparation skills using kitchen tools, recipes, and terminology before visiting a local restaurant kitchen. Teach shopping skills by visiting a supermarket and conducting comparison-shopping exercises. Make sure that field trips are well planned and barrier-free.

Cooperative Learning: By using this team approach, students with cognitive impairments are grouped with other students in your class. Cooperative grouping taps into the strengths of all students and encourages support, respect, and appreciation of others.

Graphic Organizers: Presenting information graphically allows students to understand how information relates and ideas are connected. A student's personal filing system for storing class information improves when he or she stores a graphic image along with other important information. Studies show this method is especially powerful for students with cognitive impairments/mental retardation.

Lecture Organizers: Lectures are often difficult for students with attention, processing, hearing, or cognitive impairments/mental retardation. Handing out lecture notes before speaking allows students to highlight important items while listening to the lecture. See the sample of guided notes in *Section 2*. Recording lectures allows a student to pause, replay, and slow down the information as many times as needed. Remember to use written, visual, and verbal approaches in your lectures.

Color: Add color to overheads, handouts, and the classroom to capture the students' attention. Introduce new vocabulary on different color index cards. For example, use red for types of food; blue for cooking terms; and yellow for equipment. Encourage students to use highlighters at each workstation to color-code their materials.

Procedures and Steps: Use verbal and written reminders for giving students instructions, such as cue cards or small or large posters. For example, you might use a poster that combines written instructions and pictures or symbols to present information.

Chaining: Use chaining to teach a task or technique that has multiple steps. For example, you might use chaining when teaching the steps to mixing muffins. To use chaining, go back to the first step and review all of the previous steps each time you introduce a new step in the process.

Overlearning: Overlearning gives students a chance to study and practice after achieving proficiency with course materials before you introduce new material. To ascertain their comprehension, ask students to either explain or demonstrate the concepts.

Demonstrations: Demonstrate new techniques whenever possible, emphasizing each step of the process verbally, physically, and in a handout. Incorporate as many of the senses as possible with your teaching style. Encourage students who have difficulty following the process to check off each step as you complete it. Visual and auditory learners understand information better when they hear and see it rather than only read about it. The combination of reading, hearing, and seeing is a powerful method for reaching students with cognitive impairments/mental retardation.

Breaks: Students with the need to move cannot sit still comfortably for more than 20 minutes. To accommodate this restlessness, build movement into your classroom routine every 15 to 20 minutes. Keep tasks short. Encourage students to stand to gather supplies, move to another area to watch a demonstration, or move into small groups to work on an assignment. The movement allows the students a break in the routine and a chance for their brains to process information and refocus.

Music: During silent reading or group activities, play instrumental music at 60 beats per minute. The music plays softly, becomes background noise, and assists some students with attention difficulties. Classical music and instrumental music are good choices for background noise.

Posters: Display interesting activity posters in your classroom for students to use. When working with a diverse mix of students, always use simple and clear instructions. For example, imagine you asked your students to clean the dishes after they finished cooking a meal. In an inclusive classroom, would everyone understand?

See how one student in Mrs. Ryan's class learned to use the information on the walls to help him be successful. Mrs. Ryan expects each student to participate in the team project, but not always the same job. Grades are determined by personal participation and helping other students to participate in class.

Case Study

Using Posters as Cues

Troy was excited about working in the foods lab, since foods and nutrition class was his favorite subject. Last week, Troy learned how to measure dry ingredients, so this week he volunteered to use the electric mixer to blend the dry ingredients into the creamed butter and eggs.

After mixing the ingredients, Troy volunteered to wash the dishes. Troy grabbed one of the mixing spoons and started to lick dough off the spoon. Mrs. Ryan noticed his behavior and reminded Troy that he should not eat raw dough because of possible food borne illness. She then reminded Troy about the appropriate dish-washing procedures. She pointed to the wall poster, indicating all dishes are washed in hot, soapy water, scrubbed with a dishcloth, rinsed in hot water, and dried thoroughly before being put away. The poster told Troy how to test the water to see if it is too hot or too cold. Troy put on the rubber gloves to protect his hands, followed the instructions, and avoided creating a health problem for himself and others. Remember, written and visual reminders can be helpful!

Following Up Mrs. Ryan used posters to explain health information and does not have to single anyone out. Students with cognitive impairments/mental retardation appreciate positive attention and enjoy being treated like other class members.

Quick Facts

Employment Training & Cognitive Impairment

Many large corporations, especially one-stop shopping stores, have work programs for people with disabilities. As part of their high school education, students with cognitive impairments should be taught work skills that correlate to their functioning levels. Employment training should be a collaborative effort between the school staff and local adult services agencies.

Memory Strategies: To help students increase their abilities to remember information, try the following strategies:

- Mnemonic exercises use short, common words to help low-functioning students to remember complex ideas. For example, in order to teach foodservice students how to arrange food products for dry or refrigerated storage according to date purchased, use the phrase "first in, first out" or "FIFO."
- Using rhymes, catch phrases, acronyms, word associations, and categorizations also encourages memory enhancement and retention for students with cognitive impairments/mental retardation. For example, use the catch phrase, "when in doubt, throw it out" to help students remember what to do if they doubt the safety of food.
- Using a multi-step process of association helps lower-functioning students utilize and recall information. You might use common buildings and word association to help students remember academic information. For example, most students can picture in their minds a two-story home and invent or recall vivid details about certain concepts. You might use the home example to help students remember the levels of Maslow's Hierarchy of Human Needs. See Figure 6-3 for more information.

Service Learning

Service projects help students learn about others in their community and travel beyond the walls of the classroom. *Special Olympics* offers children, students, and adults with cognitive impairments year-round training and competition in 26 Olympic-type sports. Community volunteers serve in a variety of capacities. All volunteers work together to provide the athletes with quality experiences in sports training and competition. Volunteers range from high school students to retired persons.

The following case study shows how Miss Allen includes all students. As students progress through the service learning project in her class, notice how attitudes change and friendships begin.

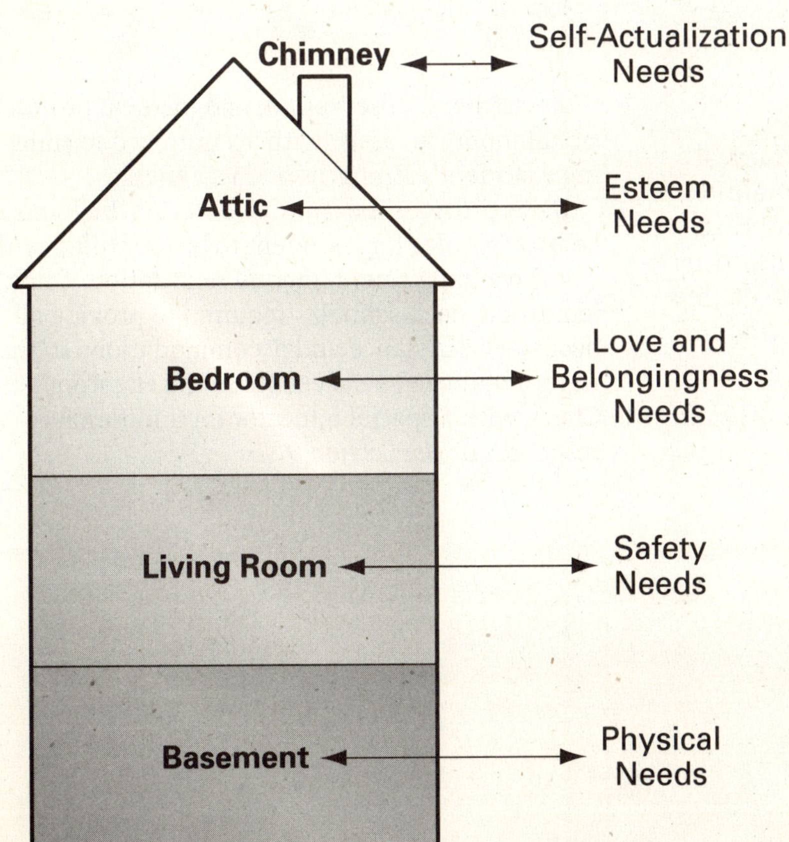

Figure 6-3 Using a multi-step process, you can help your low-functioning students to retain and utilize information. For example, using a familiar building structure, such as a house, and correlating the levels of the house to the levels in Maslow's Hierarchy of Human Needs brings together something familiar with something new.

Case Study

Special Olympics as a High School Service Project

Miss Allen announced to her class that everyone would be able to participate in the upcoming Special Olympics. Several in the class groaned, but Martin grinned because he thought this meant others would be swimming with him. Martin looked around to see who might be on his team. Two boys in the back were pointing at him with smirks on their faces. Martin smiled and waved back to them; they must be his teammates! Martin didn't understand that they would not be swimming with him—they would be coaching him.

Over the next couple of days, Miss Allen began describing cognitive impairments, discussing potential activities for involvement with the event, and answering many questions. The two boys who had snickered changed their attitudes toward Martin once they knew more about special needs. One asked to be Martin's head coach and the other his personal cheerleader. Up to that point, the students made fun of Martin because he learned much slower and his speech was unclear.

The day of the swimming event, Martin swam the race as his new coach and personal cheerleader cheered him on. What a thrill to have support and encouragement. Other classmates were timers, and some helped the winners line up to receive medals. After the event, Miss Allen led the class in a discussion about everyone's experiences. Martin's coach and personal cheerleader felt great pride—Martin had won the swim meet!

Following Up In this case study, Miss Allen captured an opportunity to teach everyone how to respect the individual gifts of those with special needs. Students learned acceptance, understanding, compassion, respect, and pride through this service learning project.

Summary

Students with cognitive impairment/mental retardation may have difficulties with attention, temporal sequential ordering, spatial ordering, memory, language, neuromotor functions, social cognition, or higher-order cognition. The degree of difficulty differs with each student. Activities must be geared to students' abilities.

Assessment, observation, and medical professional input can assist with accurately determining a student's strengths and weaknesses.

IDEA provides measurable criteria which must be met in order for a student to be identified with cognitive impairment/mental retardation. Once identified, each school is required to provide all necessary assistance and accommodations so that the student can be successful in the classroom. Check with a special educator for additional resources or see *Section 9*.

Section 7: Teaching Students with Autism and Autism Spectrum Disorders (ASD)

What is autism? According to the IDEA law, *autism* is a developmental disability (impairment) that generally appears before age three. It significantly affects a student's verbal and nonverbal communication and social interactions. It also adversely affects educational performance. Other symptoms may include:

- Abnormal emotional responses to different types of sensory stimuli, such as touch or sound.
- Impaired social skills. For example, a person with autism may resist hugging, be unable to hold a conversation, or fail to maintain eye contact with people.
- Severely limited activities and interests. Students with autism have a disrupted ability to use imagination. This symptom may be manifested in repetitive routines and behaviors, obsessive preoccupation with arranging objects, or resistance to environmental changes.

Why is it so important to understand this disability? According to the United States Department of Education, students identified with autism are increasing each year. See Figure 1-1 in *Section 1*. This 2003 report shows that in the school year of 2001-2002, students identified in the autism category increased 24 percent, while students in other disability categories increased about two percent. Because of these increasing numbers, it is vitally important for teachers, parents, psychologists, and medical personnel to work together to see that each student receives the appropriate accommodations and supports needed for school success.

Quick Facts

Autism & Immunizations

According to the most recent studies by the CDC, autism is not associated with thimerosal-containing vaccines or the MMR (Measles, Mumps, and Rubella) vaccine.

Autism Spectrum Disorders

Autism spectrum disorders (ASD) refer to the wide range of autistic characteristics that students may display. Students with ASD range from students with high intellect to students with significant cognitive impairments/mental retardation. Conditions that fit into the ASD category may include:

- **Classic Autism** (as described earlier). A small segment of this population may be diagnosed with *savant syndrome*. While functioning at a level of severe cognitive impairment in many areas, the savant may have an extraordinary gift in one area, such as the ability to perform complicated math formulas or perform music with excellence and precision.
- **Asperger Syndrome.** A student with this syndrome has average or above average intelligence, but limited social skills. These students may be naïve and lack common sense while at the same time have superior ability to remember certain information.
- **Rett Syndrome.** This is a genetic neurological disorder that primarily affects female students. After apparently normal development, students with Rett syndrome develop autism-like symptoms, such as loss of speech, reasoning, and fine- and gross-motor skills. Seizures also become more apparent as the student ages.

Students with autism or ASD vary widely in their abilities and personalities just like typical classroom students. Some may have severe cognitive impairments/mental retardation while others may show great academic success. Awareness of the symptoms can help you apply specific strategies to help your students function more successfully and achieve their IEP goals. See Figure 7-1 on page 60 for additional symptoms.

Figure 7-1

Behaviors Associated with Autism and ASD	
Behavior Type	**Symptoms of Behavior**
Communication	• Displays specific knowledge without comprehension of that knowledge. • Shows abnormalities in the ability to attend—may be attentive one moment and inattentive the next. • Difficulty focusing. Tends to focus on irrelevant stimuli. • May have superior writing skills over speaking skills. • Displays *echolalia*—mimicking the speech of others without understanding. • Displays minimal processing capabilities.
Social	• Shows difficulty in making transitions. • Displays an absence of empathy or delays in empathy. • Lacks skill in greeting people or saying good-bye. • Displays a distinctive use of vocabulary or voice. For example, students with Asperger syndrome often speak in a monotone voice.
Sensory	• Displays repetitive movements, such as hand-flapping, spinning, or rocking. • May be defensive about touch. • Displays hypersensitivity to sound, touch, visual, or auditory stimuli.
Behavioral	• Mirrors the behavior of others without comprehension of the behavior. • Needs time for task completion or closure. Student may have a negative behavioral outburst if there is not enough time to complete a task. • May display a fixation on repeating information from a story, television commercial, or movie. This may be mistaken for imaginative play. • Repetitive play, such as lining up or spinning objects. For example, a student may repetitively line up pencils or spin a pencil on the desk top.

Teaching Strategies and Accommodations for Students with Autism or ASD

Most students with autism or ASD need extra supports to function in the inclusive classroom. Here are some examples of support:

Teacher's Aide: The aide attends every class and focuses his or her support on the student with autism. This approach is helpful for the student who becomes disruptive when changes to the routine occur.

Preferential Seating: Move the student with autism to a distraction-free area. This technique allows you to redirect the student quickly when needed.

Nonverbal Signals: Use a gentle pat on the shoulder to redirect attention. This technique allows you to redirect the student without embarrassment. Use visual organizers to help with schedule predictability.

Additional Explanation: Offer additional notes or simplify abstract information. Making information more concrete allows the student with autism or ASD a better chance to grasp new information.

Chunking Assignments: This strategy involves breaking down assignments into small units with frequent teacher feedback. The student with autism becomes aware of his or her successes more frequently with this approach.

Targeting Assignments: Be sure to incorporate structured choice into your daily schedule so the student can choose what to work on. Include "high-interest" assignments.

Specialized Visual Supports: Create specialized visual supports (e.g., symbols or signs) for helping students to understand the physical layout of the classroom environment.

Class Rules: State rules in a positive manner. Declare what you want a behavior to be and then show positive examples. Affirm the student for displaying the appropriate behavior.

Buddy System: Seat a sensitive, nondisabled classmate near the student. The nondisabled student may assist the student with autism or ASD with class work or activities.

Directed Questions: Speak directly to the student with autism or ASD to help him or her attend to the lesson. Ask the student direct questions to reinforce the new materials.

Grading Assignments: Be aware that written assignments may contain repetition, jump from one subject to the next, and may use terminology incorrectly. Grade this work for content not organization.

Correcting Work: Allow poorly executed class work to be corrected. The student with autism or ASD may need a second chance to demonstrate his or her knowledge of FACS course materials.

Anger Management: Develop a list with the student's assistance of concrete steps to follow when he or she becomes upset. This is important for helping the student learn to cope with anger. Use "I" messages when talking with the student.

Noticing Changes: Report changes in the student's behavior, such as greater level of disorganization, inattentiveness, depression, or isolation to the proper staff in your school. You are important in helping to identify potential problems.

The extra support you provide often assists the student with the positive feedback and the redirection he or she requires. If you have difficulty teaching a student with autism, contact a special educator. Many districts have specialists or special resource centers that have personnel to assist teachers with low-incidence disabilities such as autism or ASD.

When the student with autism interacts with other students in your class, he or she is learning to negotiate the world around him or her.
Be sure you celebrate the small victories these students make in meeting their goals. Continue to increase the level of expectations you have of them to help them achieve more.

In the following case study, Sandy learns how to use her encyclopedic mind to assist with a project. By pairing Sandy with another student, Mrs. Kim allows each student to be successful and gain recognition for the work performed.

Case Study

Knowing the Right Information Helps a Student with Autism

Sandy often talked about her fish tank so much her depth of knowledge bored others. Sandy wanted others to like her, but she did not understand that not everyone was interested in her favorite subject. Students often made fun of her behind her back and cracked jokes she could not understand. Sandy thought the attention was positive and smiled back at the students.

Mrs. Kim noticed the behavior and paired Sandy with an understanding student during the research phase of the foods class. Sandy and her partner decided to explore why eating fish was good for your health. The two students read books, encyclopedias, and browsed the Internet looking for information. Sandy easily memorized her portion of the information. During the presentation, Sandy talked about what she had learned and her partner explained why the information was important. Using this approach, Sandy was able to use her encyclopedic memory and avoid the higher-order skills needed to interpret the knowledge.

Following Up Mrs. Kim understood Sandy's disability enough to know that if she asked Sandy to talk about fish, Sandy could talk proudly about her knowledge. Helping Sandy talk about the right subject made all the difference in building her self-esteem.

Additional Support Therapies

Students with autism or ASD may receive additional supports to manage their lives. These additional supports are generally outlined in the student's IEP.

Sensory Integration Therapy: Sensory integration is the ability to take in and process sensory information in order to make appropriate adaptive responses. Students who have problems integrating sensations may be over- or under-reactive to touch, movement, sounds, or visual information. They may have unusually high or low activity levels. A student with disordered sensory integration may have problems with learning, development, or behavior. Sensory integration therapy focuses on touch, how the inner ear responds to head/body movements, and muscles and joints in relation to body awareness.

Auditory Integration Training (AIT): A student with autism or ASD may be hypersensitive (oversensitive) or hyposensitive (tuned out) to sound. Auditory integration therapy attempts to improve, strengthen, or exercise the acoustic reflex muscle in the middle ear. By this process, therapists hope to see improvement in the student's bodily reaction to sensory overload (or sound) in the brain.

Music Therapy: In order to eliminate the pain from certain sound frequencies, a student with autism or ASD may shut down his or her hearing to avoid hearing certain sounds. This may cause sounds to be heard incorrectly and interpreted incorrectly. Music therapy helps improve a student's hearing with the use of music. Music is motivating and enjoyable and promotes relaxation, learning, and self-expression. The natural components of music, such as the structure and sensory elements, help establish positive interactions and organization.

Speech/Language Therapy: Often a student with autism or ASD will work with a speech therapist to improve his or her speech or language ability. The therapist may help students learn to put sentences together using scripts, pictures, or videos. The student receives instruction about appropriate behaviors when reviewing the tapes with the therapist. Students with autism that do not talk may use other communication strategies, such as:

- American Sign Language (ASL).
- Augmentative and Alternative Communication (AAC).

See *Section 5* for more information on ASL and AAC.

Art Therapy: With the use of art materials and the processes used in creating art, art therapists work with students with autism or ASD to help them overcome their social isolation and gain a sense of self and how they relate to the world. Art therapy also encourages communication by expression with art materials. As with other therapies, a consistent place and time helps encourage relationships.

There are some additional accepted strategies and therapies that are used with students with autism or ASD. These skill-based strategies are not generally used in the inclusive classroom, but may be used by therapists and special educators when working with these students. See Figure 7-2 on page 63 for information on these strategies.

With autism or ASD, a student's true intellectual ability may be unknown. This has important implications for the student who will soon leave high school and go into the job market. High expectations, patience, and acceptance of the student's gifts go a long way toward helping others see the student as a whole person.

The following case study shows an adult with autism working successfully at a daily job. Accommodations occur, but she definitely has a career.

CASE STUDY

Autism in the Workplace

Nina works in the microfilming section of her county services department. She lifts sacks of mail, places the mail into the correct bins, loads a cart, and delivers the mail and packages to the proper departments within her building. A true member of the working force, she collects a union wage, carries medical insurance, pays taxes, and pays for her job coach with her own earnings. Nina's job coach is an employee that Nina hires and pays from a combination of her own earnings and a government program called Impairment Related Work Expense (IRWE). The IRWE program is run by the Social Security Administration to assist people with disabilities so they may have the supports they need to work competitively.

Following Up Nina has held this job for the past eight years and has earned the respect of those around her. She was taught how to use sign language when she was 4 years old and communicates using the 50 words she has learned. No one knows all the abilities that Nina has because autism keeps her abilities hidden. Imagine the pride Nina feels in being a full member of society.

Figure 7-2

Skill-Based Strategies for Students with Autism or ASD

The following strategies are universally accepted techniques for working with students with autism or ASD. It may be likely that you will hear about these strategies at a student's IEP meeting. These strategies require specialized training and generally involve therapists and special educators.

ABA (Applied Behavior Analysis)	Developed at the University of California—Los Angeles, ABA is a systematic behavioral approach to teaching students with autism or ASD. These students are often resistant to change and often respond best when a routine is repeated on a daily basis. The six features of ABA include: 1. Define the new skill or behavior to be learned. 2. Measure the student's performance of the skill frequently. 3. Provide opportunities for the student to actively respond during instruction. 4. Provide immediate feedback on student performance with correction or reinforcement. 5. Transfer the teacher prompts to naturally occurring prompts or self-initiated prompts. 6. Create strategies for maintaining the newly acquired behavior without teacher prompts.
DTT (Discrete Trial Training)	This is a behavioral technique that teaches a skill in very small units or trials. The trial typically consists of instruction given in a clear, concise manner; a response by the student; and followed by feedback from the teacher.
TEACCH (Treatment and Education of Autistic and related Communication handicapped CHildren)	Developed at the University of North Carolina—Chapel Hill, the TEACCH program focuses on the individualized assessment of a person with autism or ASD and develops a program based on this person's skills, interests, and needs. Structured teaching is a key element in the TEACCH program. It involves organizing a student's physical environment, developing effective schedules, giving clear and explicit expectations, and the use of visual materials. This system allows students to use their skills without teacher prompts or cues.
PECS (Picture Exchange Communication System)	Used initially at the Delaware Autistic Program (co-developed by Andrew S. Bondy and Lori A. Frost), in this strategy, teachers and students with autism or ASD use symbols and pictures to communicate. The pictures are exchanged for an item being requested. For example, a picture of a mixing spoon is redeemed for the actual mixing spoon. By high school, these students generally have learned some vocabulary or use of assistive technology to help them communicate. At the high school level, PECS may be used in conjunction with other methods to teach students effectively.

Summary

Students with autism or ASD are a small, but growing, population. Many times, a student's abilities are unknown. Some students with autism or ASD have learned to communicate at very high levels through extensive therapies and augmentative or alternative communication devices. However, many students with autism or ASD are often unable to effectively communicate their needs and wants. These students may have significant cognitive impairments or may have high intellect. This population of students needs the respect, consideration, and opportunities presented in the FACS classroom.

See *Section 9* for resources that may be helpful in learning more about autism and ASD.

Section 8: Fostering Self-Determination and Self-Advocacy

Since teens are transitioning between childhood and adulthood, high school is a time when they are trying to discover what the world holds for their futures. A number of issues face teens these days including high stakes assessment, peer pressure regarding sexuality/sexual development, and social skills. The FACS curriculum is designed to assist students in gaining the knowledge, skills, and attitudes to successfully embrace the adult roles they choose. Teaching students to become self-determined and independent improves post-school outcomes.

More and more high school students are participating in their own IEP meetings. By law, students must be invited to participate in the IEP meeting if transition services will be discussed. As students prepare to transition into adult roles as college students or workers, they need to understand how their disabilities will impact their performance in their future adult roles. By participating in their IEP meetings, students gain important information about the goal-setting and accommodation processes.

In the case study that follows, Jenny is a great example of a student who is self-determined and self-directed. She knows what she wants, understands her limitations, and will be her own advocate to obtain the supports that she needs.

Case Study

Jenny Runs Her Own IEP Meeting

Jenny opened her IEP meeting by introducing everyone: "Hello, Mrs. King, I'd like you to meet my mother, Mrs. Vine." Jenny went around the room introducing each participant to her mother and explained each person's role at school.

Jenny announced that she wanted to share a PowerPoint® presentation that she had made in her Life Skills class. "This presentation will help us plan my education program for next year. I'd like to share a little bit about where I've been and where I want to go." As Jenny clicked through the slides she narrated, "When I was six years old, the doctors at Children's Hospital saved my life. The illness I had hurt my vision and my hearing. So now I have to wear these thick glasses and a hearing aid."

Then Jenny showed her IEP team some pictures in high school. "Here is a picture of me busing tables at Sandy's Grille. I hated working with dirty dishes in a restaurant. Here is another photo at the Community Services Center where I volunteered to help with the elderly. It was hard for me to hear what they were saying!" Next, Jenny showed a slide that summarized the results of two interest inventories that she took. Both inventories supported a career goal of working with computers.

"I love working with computers. I can adjust the computer to accommodate my disability so my vision and hearing are not problems. I'd like to be a graphic communications designer. This year I need to focus on passing my math proficiency assessment. A final slide was a photo showing Jenny in her ideal work situation—working on computers.

Jenny's IEP team congratulated Jenny on her excellent presentation. They discussed strategies to help Jenny pass her math proficiency assessment and apply to the local community college for an associate degree in graphic communications. Together, the IEP team and Jenny mapped out the plans to help her accomplish her career goal.

Following Up Mrs. King, Jenny's Life Skills teacher, provided her with teaching materials and resources to further her self-determination skills. Throughout the class, Jenny researched her career goals, worked and volunteered in several jobs, became aware of how her disability impacted her performance in different work settings, and developed her presentation skills.

What Is Self-Determination?

Self-determination is defined as a combination of skills, knowledge, and beliefs that enables a person to engage in goal-directed, self-regulated behavior. Self-determined people know what they want, choose goals, and pursue them.

Self-determination involves students' assertiveness in making their needs known by developing self-advocacy skills, evaluating progress toward meeting their goals, adjusting their performance, and creating unique approaches to solve problems. According to the researchers Wehmeyer and Schwartz, students who develop self-determination skills have a greater chance for achieving positive post-school outcomes.

Many professionals recommend that students have multiple opportunities to experience success on many levels, which over time enhances their self-determination. Some students with disabilities do not learn self-advocacy or self-determination skills because parents and teachers are constantly controlling their environment and meeting all of their needs. For students to develop self-determination, they must be able to make their own choices. You can facilitate these skills by building many opportunities for decision making into your classes. Allowing students to experience the natural consequences of their decisions teaches them important lessons.

In the following case study, see how two teachers teamed up to integrate their curricula to teach self-determination in context of career exploration, goal setting, and reading, writing, and research skills. Together, these two teachers taught the mandated academic standards, while designing a relevant and engaging project. Students were empowered to work harder because the final class presentation was in front of their peers. They could use posters, media, and technology to present their final projects. They learned more about different career requirements and college majors by listening to each other's self-directed career presentations.

The innovative teachers in the case study found that by integrating self-determination and career exploration into their classes, students were able to see the correlation between the curriculum and their own personal lives. English skills became more relevant.

The teachers provided opportunities to use self-guided practice skills to assist students in learning how large goals should be for the first week. Students were able to apply the objectives of the reading and writing assignments to their own life experiences. The literature had "real life" implications and students were able to write about the relevance to their own lives. As students set short-term goals, they had support from their teachers and peers. Students became comfortable setting goals that were reasonable and asked for assistance when needed.

What Is Self-Advocacy?

Self-advocacy means speaking up for yourself by expressing your needs and desires to function as an independent adult. Students with disabilities, just as their nondisabled peers, do not know how to be self-advocates. The first step in becoming self-advocates is for students to learn about themselves. What are their strengths and weaknesses? Students should understand how they learn, what they are good at, what their goals are, and what types of supports they need to accomplish their goals successfully. Students who know how and when to ask for help accomplish their goals and are more self-determined. Teachers can teach and reinforce these skills every day through the FACS curricula.

Some questions that teachers can ask their students to get them thinking about self-advocacy include:

Do You...

- Know what you're good at?
- Know how to ask for support?

Case Study

Integrating Self-Determination into Inclusive Careers and English Classrooms

Miss Williams, the FACS Careers teacher, and Mr. Hart, the English teacher, team teach an inclusive group of ninth graders. As high school teachers, they are responsible for meeting the Language Arts standards that include reading comprehension—both written and oral communication skills—and research skills. The majority of ninth grade students must demonstrate proficiency of these standards by passing a state-mandated "Ninth-Grade Proficiency Assessment."

Miss Williams and Mr. Hart integrated a unit on self-determination and transition planning into their classroom. The teachers had three goals: build upon a foundation of self-exploration, self-awareness, and self-evaluation; teach students how to set goals, develop short-term objectives, and implement and monitor their own plans; and provide students with an opportunity to present their career projects. Miss Williams and Mr. Hart used literature to provide positive examples and non-examples of characters who demonstrated (or failed to demonstrate) self-determination. For example:

- In the book *The Giver* by Lois Lowry, the high school students in the book were given a career based on the observations of adults. The main character, Jonas, was unhappy with his assigned career and questioned this practice. The character was not allowed to be self-determined.

As students worked through their own career exploration activities, Miss Williams and Mr. Hart had students compare and contrast their own lives to the lives of the characters.

Students were then asked to develop a presentation that outlined the following points:

- A summary of their likes, dislikes, and dreams for their futures.
- The results of several interest surveys and personality and learning style inventories that asked students to evaluate their own skills related to transition.
- A summary of the strengths and the skills they needed to improve to reach their goals.
- Written education and career goals with written plans that outline the activities to implement in order to meet each goal.

Following Up Students took turns presenting their plans to their classmates. They learned a lot about different career paths and college requirements by listening to each other. Students who had IEPs made their presentations to their IEP teams. Parents and teachers were impressed by these students' presentations, that IEP meetings ran more smoothly, and that expectations for student performance were raised. Parents had a better understanding of the transition statements and students had more ownership of their IEPs.

- Understand your strengths and challenges?
- Know your rights?
- Share your ideas with others?
- Learn new skills from others?
- Speak up to others about your needs?
- Feel good about yourself?
- Tell your friends how you feel?
- Tell your friends what you think?

Once students become aware of the benefits of self-advocacy skills, you can encourage them to get the facts about their interests and the ways that they best learn. Once they have the facts, encourage them to start small, with one goal at a time. Encourage students to begin with a goal that they can accomplish within a week so that they quickly experience some success. In the case study on page 67, see how Mrs. Vance helped Matthew self-advocate in her class.

Case Study

Matthew Speaks Up

Mrs. Vance observed the small group in the corner. Matthew looked really unhappy. The other team members were talking as they followed the recipe. Matthew was washing the vegetables for the salad.

Mrs. Vance called Matthew over to her desk. She asked: "Matthew, what's the matter. Why do you look so upset?" Matthew replied, "The other team members won't let me read the recipe because I read slowly. They told me that I had to wash vegetables again. I'm tired of always doing the same thing. I want to cook."

Mrs. Vance explained to Matthew that the cooking jobs are supposed to be rotated. "That's one of the class rules—that no one does the same job over and over." Mrs. Vance suggested that Matthew go back to his team and tell them that he wants to sauté the vegetables this week. Matthew said that he was uncomfortable telling his team what he wanted to do. Mrs. Vance and Matthew practiced until he felt comfortable. After a couple of role-plays, Matthew said he was ready—he walked back to his team and said: "I'd like to sauté the vegetables today. Our team grade will be better if we rotate all the different cooking jobs." His classmates agreed. Matthew smiled as he began to stir the vegetables in the pan.

Following Up Mrs. Vance could have intervened and reminded Matthew's team that their team grade was dependent on everyone rotating the cooking tasks; however, she knew that Matthew could advocate for himself with a little bit of encouragement and practice. Matthew learned that instead of pouting in the corner of the class, he needed to speak up for himself.

Communicating Effectively

Students with disabilities need to communicate effectively to coordinate accommodations and supports. It is important to teach students how to advocate within the classroom and use appropriate communication styles. In order for students to become strong self-advocates, they need to learn how to be effective communicators. See Figure 8-2 for three types of communication. The lesson plan that follows in Figure 8-3 on page 68 suggests procedures to teach effective communication skills using the three types of communication in Figure 8-2.

Figure 8-2

Types of Communication

Passive Communication

- Uses a soft speaking voice.
- Reluctantly expresses needs.
- Lacks skill in persisting to get needs addressed.

Aggressive Communication

- Uses a loud speaking voice; can be angry and/or physical when speaking.
- Uses intimidation and tends to be overdemanding or overbearing.
- Does not listen well; undermines teamwork.
- Tends to promote hostile relationships.

Assertive Communication

- Knows his or her own goals.
- Uses a medium speaking voice.
- Makes a request or suggestion, rather than a demand or threat.
- Shows appreciation to people for listening and for their support.
- Promotes teamwork.

Figure 8-3

Lesson Plan for Learning Different Types of Communication

1. Discuss the different types of communication listed in Figure 8-2. Compare and contrast the behavioral patterns of the three types of communication. Ask pairs of students to role-play the different types of communication or model each style yourself and ask the students to identify the type (passive, aggressive, or assertive). Create a handout of the information in Figure 8-2 for students to use with Steps 3 and 4.
2. If students work in pairs to model the different types of communication, cut strips of paper and write one type of communication on each strip. There should be enough strips listing the three types of communication (passive, aggressive, and assertive) for each pair of students to draw one strip.
3. Divide the class into pairs. Ask each pair to draw a strip listing one of the types of communication. Direct the pairs to develop a role-play that depicts the type of communication pattern on their slips. Students with a slip listing Assertive Communication should demonstrate the Behaviors of Assertive Communication. Pairs depicting Aggressive Communication and Passive Communication should demonstrate the behavior patterns describing their type of communication. Give them enough time to plan their role-plays and practice.
4. Each pair is then asked to act out their communication role-play for the group. The remainder of the class is asked to identify the communication pattern presented using the handout on the three types of communication provided earlier. The pairs representing Aggressive Communication and Passive Communication are asked what they need to do differently to become assertive communicators. Those pairs representing Assertive Communication are asked how many of the behaviors they demonstrated.

Teaching effective communication styles is fun. Students like role-plays and it is a very effective teaching method. Teach communication styles early in the school year and then reinforce students throughout the year to use their "assertive communication style" when working as a team.

Summary

Educators face many challenges in determining how to balance academic content standards and state assessments with the development of self-determination skills, self-advocacy skills, and transition services. Both the IDEA and No Child Left Behind laws emphasize student involvement and progress in all these areas.

As educators, you must assure that the skills students need to succeed are indeed taught through your curricula with special education supports. Each student's educational program must include content on self-determination, self-advocacy, and career development skills.

To the extent possible, students must use their self-advocacy skills to coordinate the accommodations they need in high school so that they are more prepared to act independently in post-high school settings, such as college, employment, and independent living.

Section 9: Web Resources

The following Web sites are sources that you can use to find additional information about many of the topics discussed in this booklet. The following Web sites are organized by sections of this booklet.

Section 1—FACS Skills for All Learners

All Kinds of Minds

www.allkindsofminds.org

All Kinds of Minds is a nonprofit institute for understanding the learning differences in students. The mission for this organization is to, "help students who struggle with learning measurably improve their success in school and life by providing programs that integrate educational, scientific and clinical expertise."

Brain Gym

www.braingym.org

Brain Gym exercises prepare the brain for learning. This Web site discusses how the exercises provide "often dramatic improvements in concentration, memory, reading, organization skills, language and number skills, writing, speaking, athletic performance, and more."

Buzan Centres

www.mind-map.com

Mind mapping® is a visual organizational technique. The Web site describes how to draw maps and where to locate resources for learning about the techniques. .

Kids Quest, National Center for Birth Defects and Developmental Disabilities

www.cdc.gov/ncbddd/kids

This Web site is dedicated to explaining disabilities to students. Quizzes, games, and information are woven together to explain terminology to students.

Music in the Classroom

www.musicintheclassroom.com

This Web site describes why 60 beats per minute music is important for students with disabilities.

Partnership for Learning

http://www.partnershipforlearning.org

The Partnership for Learning is a nonprofit group for "equipping families and communities to maximize learning." The Partnership provides publications, speakers, collaboration assistance, literacy training and activities, and media support.

Schools Attuned

www.schoolsattuned.org

This Web site is filled with ideas for educators. It is provided by All Kinds of Minds to manage information about students with differences in learning.

Schwab Learning

http://www.schwablearning.org

Schwab Learning is a nonprofit foundation that provides publications, information, resources and support to families who have children with challenges related to learning.

U.S. Department of Education

www.ed.gov

With details on grants and contracts, financial aid, research and statistics, policy and programs, the United States Department of Education Web site promotes quality education for everyone. Information for students, parents, teachers, and administrators about legislation, requirements, and definitions can be found here.

Section 2—Meeting the Needs of All Learners

Center for Applied Special Technology (CAST)

www.cast.org

CAST is a not-for-profit organization that uses technology to expand opportunities for all people, especially those with disabilities. The Association for Supervision and Curriculum Development (ASCD) book "Teaching Every Student in the Digital Age: Universal Design for Learning" is available in electronic form at CAST's Web site.

Fast Facts for Faculty Series

http://www.osu.edu/grants/dpg/fastfact/notes.html

Guided notes: Improving the effectiveness of your lectures is available online. By offering a description, benefits, FAQs, and guidelines, this Web site discusses how to use guided notes.

Fast Facts for Faculty Series: Universal Design for Learning: Elements of Good Teaching

http://www.osu.edu/grants/dpg/fastfact/undesign.html

This Web site discusses elements for good teaching.

National Center to Improve Practice (NCIP) in Special Education Through Technology, Media and Materials

http://www2.edc.org/NCIP/Default.htm

Through offerings like online workshops and events, the NCIP library, and video profiles, the center promotes "the effective use of assistive and instructional technologies among educators and related personnel" serving students with disabilities.

Section 3—Special Education Policies and Practices

Council for Exceptional Children (CEC)

www.cec.sped.org

The CEC focuses on improving educational outcomes for students with disabilities.

Families and Advocates Partnership for Education

www.FAPE.org

This organization helps connect families and advocates improving the education of students with disabilities.

ILIAD and ASPIIRE IDEA Partnership Projects

www.ideapractices.org

This Web site offers information about IDEA of 1997 and answers many questions, such as how the law will help children with disabilities reach their fullest potential.

Educating Students with Disabilities in the Least Restrictive Environment

http://www.nysut.org/research/bulletins/20020816leastrestrictiveenvironment.html

This bulletin by the New York State United Teachers gives an overview of "Least Restrictive Environment" and covers inclusion as well as considering how the concepts can be implemented.

National Dissemination Center for Children and Youth with Disabilities (NICHCY)

www.nichcy.org

This Web site is responsible for disseminating information on IDEA.

U.S. Department of Education

www.ed.gov

This Web site provides information about current legislation, such as the IDEA of 1997, as well as information about current department offices and initiatives.

Section 4—Teaching Students with Invisible Disabilities

Children and Adults with Attention-Deficit/Hyperactivity Disorder (CHADD)

www.chadd.org

CHADD is the nation's leading nonprofit organization serving individuals with AD/HD.

Learning Disabilities Association of America (LDA)

www.ldanatl.org

The Learning Disabilities Association of America (LDA) is a nonprofit grassroots organization whose members are individuals with learning disabilities, their families, and the professionals who work with them. LDA strives to advance the education and general welfare of children and adults with learning disabilities.

National Attention Deficit Disorder Association (ADDA)

www.add.org

ADDA provides information, resources, and networking opportunities to help adults with Attention Deficit/Hyperactivity Disorder (AD/HD) lead better lives.

National Center on Accessing the General Curriculum

http://www.cast.org/ncac/

The National Center on Accessing the General Curriculum provides a vision of how new curricula, teaching practices, and policies can be woven together to create practical approaches for improved access to the general curriculum by students with disabilities.

National Institute of Mental Health (NIMH)

www.nimh.nih.gov

The mission of NIMH is to reduce the burden of mental illness and behavioral disorders through research on mind, brain, and behavior.

Section 5—Teaching Students with Sensory, Orthopedic, and Other Health Impairments

American Epilepsy Society

http://www.aesnet.org/

The American Epilepsy Society offers many member services including research, education, and publications.

Council for Exceptional Children (CEC)

www.cec.sped.org

The CEC focuses on improving educational outcomes for students with disabilities.

Cystic Fibrosis Foundation

http://www.cff.org/

The Cystic Fibrosis Foundation is a resource of information about cystic fibrosis. It is dedicated to the development of the means to cure and control cystic fibrosis and improve the quality of life for those with the disease.

National Association of the Deaf

http://www.nad.org/about/index.html

The National Association of the Deaf focuses on safeguarding the rights of the deaf and hard of hearing in regard to education, employment, health care, and telecommunication. It offers resources on issues related to the deaf and hearing impaired including American Sign Language (ASL).

National Federation of the Blind

http://www.nfb.org

With fifty thousand members, the NFB has affiliates in all fifty states plus Washington, D.C. and Puerto Rico, and over seven hundred local chapters. As a consumer and advocacy organization, the NFB is considered the leading force in the blindness field today.

The American Diabetes Association

http://www.diabetes.org/home.jsp

The American Diabetes Association provides diabetes research, information, and advocacy. Its mission is to prevent and cure diabetes and improve the lives of all people affected by diabetes.

The National Spinal Cord Injury Association

http://www.spinalcord.org/html/about.php

The National Spinal Cord Injury Association is dedicated to improving the quality of life for Americans living with the results of spinal cord injury. It offers an innovative peer support network and educational awareness.

United Cerebral Palsy

http://www.ucp.org

United Cerebral Palsy is a leading information source that strives to advance opportunities for people with cerebral palsy and other disabilities.

Section 6—Teaching Students with Cognitive Impairments/ Mental Retardation

All Kinds of Minds

www.allkindsofminds.org

The mission for this organization is to "help students who struggle with learning measurably improve their success in school and life by providing programs that integrate educational, scientific and clinical expertise."

American Association of Mental Retardation

www.aamr.org

This Web site provides services and resources for individuals with mental retardation.

Brain Gym

www.braingym.org

This Web site discusses how brain exercises provide "often dramatic improvements in concentration, memory, reading, organization skills, language and number skills, writing, speaking, athletic performance, and more."

Council for Exceptional Children (CEC)

www.cec.sped.org

The CEC focuses on improving educational outcomes for students with disabilities.

Kids Quest, National Center on Birth Defects and Developmental Disabilities

www.cdc.gov/ncbddd/kids

This Web site is dedicated to explaining disabilities to students. Quizzes, games, and information are woven together to explain terminology to students.

National Service-Learning Clearinghouse (NSLC)

http://www.servicelearning.org

The clearinghouse Web site features basic information, hot topics, a library as well as resources and tools pertaining to service learning.

Special Olympics

www.specialolympics.org

Special Olympics is an international organization dedicated to helping everyone understand mental retardation. This Web site contains many ideas for teachers on how to discuss mental retardation within the classroom.

The ARC

www.thearc.org

This Web site provides information for all children and adults with cognitive, intellectual, and developmental disabilities in every community.

The Early Learning Site

http://aba.insightcommerce.net

The Early Learning Site is dedicated to working with students who have autism. Products, suggestions, and teaching tips provide ideas for all who are learning about autism.

U.S. Department of Education

www.ed.gov

This Web site promotes quality education for everyone. Information about legislation, requirements, and definitions can be found here.

Section 7—Teaching Students with Autism and Autism Spectrum Disorders (ASD)

Council for Exceptional Children (CEC)

www.cec.sped.org

The CEC focuses on improving educational outcomes for students with disabilities.

Cure Autism Now

http://www.canfoundation.org/

Cure Autism Now is a foundation of parents, clinicians, and scientists committed to "accelerating the pace of biomedical research in autism through research, education and outreach."

Easter Seals

http://www.easterseals.com

Easter Seals offers assistance with medical rehabilitation, early intervention, therapy, job training and employment, child care, adult day services, camping and recreation, and advocacy.

MAAP Services for the Autism and Asperger Syndrome

http://www.maapservices.org

This nonprofit organization, through its newsletter, printed materials, information network, and presentations, strives to support those interacting with advanced individuals within the autism spectrum.

National Autistic Society

www.nas.org.uk.

This organization supports families with autism by helping them locate and receive services.

Online Asperger Syndrome Information and Support

www.udel.edu/bkirby/asperger

This Web site is dedicated to parents and family members of students with Asperger Syndrome.

The Autism Society of America

http://www.autism-society.org

This organization promotes "lifelong access and opportunity for all individuals within the autism spectrum, and their families, to be fully participating, included members of their community."

Section 8—Fostering Self-Determination & Self-Advocacy

Center on Self-Determination

http://cdrc.ohsu.edu/selfdetermination/about/index.html

The Center on Self-Determination identifies, develops, and shares approaches that promote the self-determination of people with disabilities and ongoing health conditions.

Council for Exceptional Children (CEC)

www.cec.sped.org

The CEC focuses on improving educational outcomes for students with disabilities.

National Center for Secondary Education and Transition (NCSET)

www.ncset.org

NCSET coordinates national resources, offers technical assistance, and disseminates information related to secondary education and transition for youth with disabilities in order to create opportunities for youth with disabilities to achieve successful futures.

National Collaborative on Workforce and Disability

http://www.ncwd-youth.info/success_Stories/index.html

NCWD/Youth is a source for information about employment and youth with disabilities. NCWD has experts in disability, education, employment, and workforce development. Read about student success stories as students with disabilities gain quality education and transition services that connect them to employment.

Self-Determination and the Education of Students with Disabilities

http://ericec.org/digests/e632.html

This online digest by The ERIC Clearinghouse on Disabilities and Gifted Education describes self-determination, why it is important, and how it can be promoted at various academic levels.

The Transition Center at the University of Florida

http://www.thetransitioncenter.org

With information for students, families, professionals, and visitors, the mission of The Transition Center is "to serve as a catalyst for coordination of research, education, and service relating to adolescents and adults, especially those with disabilities, as they make and act upon community, employment, and personal/social choices."

Additional Resources

Creating Mentoring Opportunities for Youth with Disabilities: Issues and Suggested Strategies

http://www.ncset.org/publications/viewdesc.asp?id=704

This publication by the National Center on Secondary Education and Transition describes types of mentoring and its benefits, poses questions for consideration, and suggests ways to make mentoring accessible.

Disability Mentoring Day

http://www.dmd-aapd.org

Disability Mentoring Day is "a partnership between the American Association of People with Disabilities (AAPD) and the U.S. Department of Labor Office of Disability Employment Policy (ODEP)." The event centers on job-shadowing opportunities.

International Dyslexia Association (IDA)

http://www.interdys.org

With information compiled for educators, parents, adults, college students, and children of all ages, this nonprofit is "dedicated to helping individuals with dyslexia, their families, and the communities that support them."

Job Accommodation Network (JAN)

http://www.dol.gov/odep/programs/job.htm

This network is a program of the U.S. Department of Labor's Office of Disability Employment Policy. It is a toll-free information and referral service on job accommodations for people with disabilities; on the employment provisions of the Americans with Disabilities Act; and on resources for technical assistance, funding, education, and services related to the employment of people with disabilities.

NEA: IDEA Briefs

http://www.nea.org/specialed/allbriefs.html

These documents use the question-and-answer format to explain developments related to the Individuals with Disabilities Education Act.

The Brain Injury Association of America

http://www.biausa.org

The association is a nonprofit organization dedicated to helping people with brain injuries and their families through its clearinghouse of information and resources.

The Down Syndrome Information Network

http://www.down-syndrome.info

For families, professionals, and researchers studying Down syndrome, this Web site aims to support, inform, foster communication, and enhance public understanding of the condition, "the most common cause of developmental disability."

The Epilepsy Foundation

http://www.epilepsyfoundation.org

With more than 60 affiliated foundations, The Epilepsy Foundation has a mission "to work for children and adults affected by seizures through research, education, advocacy and service."

The National Down Syndrome Society

http://www.ndss.org

Education, research, and advocacy are the three components of the NDSS mission. The society aims to be the national leader helping people with Down syndrome reach their fullest potential.

Tourette Syndrome Association, Inc.

http://www.tsa-usa.org

The TSA is a nonprofit organization working to identify the cause of, find the cure for, and control the effects of Tourette syndrome. It offers educational materials, coordinates support services and funds research. The association's Web site includes a section on education and advocacy programs as well as an information area for kids.

Chapter 1 Activity Plan: Consumer Powers & Protections

Objective: To understand the powers and protections consumers have.

Teaching Activity

1 Have students work in small groups to brainstorm the rights and responsibilities they have as consumers, workers, and citizens. On a large piece of tag board, have students list the rights and responsibilities associated with each of these roles. Have each group share its list with the class.

Accommodations/Modifications

- Invite a local government official, such as the mayor, county board president, or city council member, to the classroom to discuss citizen responsibilities. (ADD, ADHD, BD, EBD, ED, ELL, FAS, HI, LD, MR, OHI, OI, SLD, TBI, VI)
- Provide students with examples of rights and responsibilities and have students identify them as belonging to consumers, workers, and citizens. (ADD, ADHD, ASD, ELL, FAS, LD, MR, SLD, TBI)
- Have students interview adults to find out what they see as their rights and responsibilities as consumers, workers, and citizens. (ADD, ADHD, BD, EBD, ED, LD, SLD)
- Have students make a video for middle-schoolers to demonstrate consumer, worker, and citizen rights and responsibilities. (ADD, ADHD, BD, EBD, ED, LD, SLD, TBI)

Teaching Activity

2 Have students work in small groups to design a portrait of an effective consumer. Have the groups trace a full-size body silhouette on a large piece of paper and fill the image with pictures, words, and drawings that portray an effective consumer. Each group should share its finished image with the class. Post the images in the classroom as a reminder of the characteristics of an effective consumer.

Accommodations/Modifications

- Provide students with examples of effective consumers and ineffective consumers. Have students categorize the examples. (ASD, BD, ELL, FAS, MR, TBI)
- Have students use the computer to design a similar project. (ADD, ADHD, BD, EBD, ED, OHI, OI)
- Have students describe an effective consumer verbally or in writing. (ASD, ELL, HI, VI)
- Have students work with a partner for this activity. (ASD, FAS, LD, MR, OHI, OI, SLD, TBI)

Continued on next page

Teaching Activity

3 Have each student select a product he or she is interested in purchasing and research it in *Consumer Reports* magazine. Then have students choose which brand of the product they would purchase, based on the information gained through their research. Have them make a poster about their item, explaining its features and other factors to consider before purchasing the item. Have students present their posters to the rest of the class and display them in the classroom.

Accommodations/Modifications

- ◆ Provide students with reports about a particular product. (ADD, ADHD, BD, EBD, ED, ELL, LD, SLD)
- ◆ Visit a technology or an appliance retail store with students. Have a sales associate describe the differences between similar products. (ADD, ADHD, ASD, BD, EBD, ED, ELL, FAS, HI, LD, MR, OHI, OI, SLD, TBI, VI)
- ◆ Have students work with a partner for this activity. (ASD, ELL, FAS, LD, MR, OHI, SLD, TBI)

Teaching Activity

4 Have each student develop an educational project to inform others about how to prevent identity theft and what to do if their identity is stolen. Students could develop newsletter articles, electronic slide presentations, brochures, and so on. Students should use the textbook and reputable online resources to gather information for the project. Some online sources include the following:

- The Federal Trade Commission at http://www.consumer.gov/idtheft/.
- Rutgers Cooperative Extension at www.rce.rutgers.edu/Money/identitytheft/.
- Utah State Extension at http://extension.usu.edu/files/factsheets/preventing_identity_theft.pdf.
- Colorado State Cooperative Extension at www.ext.colostate.edu/pubs/columnym/ym505.html.

Have students present their projects to school and community groups, publish their articles in a school or community newsletter, or distribute printed materials to community members.

Accommodations/Modifications

- ◆ Have students work with a partner for this activity. (ASD, ELL, FAS, MR, TBI)
- ◆ Have students use assistive technology or software templates to complete this activity. (ADD, ADHD, BD, EBD, ED, HI, MR, OHI, OI, TBI, VI)
- ◆ Provide students with examples or ideas for projects. (ADD, ADHD, BD, EBD, ED, LD, SLD)
- ◆ View television commercials that warn consumers about identity theft. (ADD, ADHD, BD, EBD, ED, ELL, FAS, LD, MR, OHI, OI, SLD, TBI)

Continued on next page

Teaching Activity

5 Have students use the Better Business Bureau Web site http://www.bbb.org/ to locate consumer information about particular stores or businesses. Students could investigate both national and state consumer claims. Lead a discussion about how the Better Business Bureau or similar agencies help protect consumers.

Accommodations/Modifications

- Visit the Chamber of Commerce for students to learn more about the businesses in their area. (ADD, ADHD, ASD, BD, EBD, ED, ELL, FAS, HI, LD, MR, OHI, OI, SLD, TBI, VI)
- Have students role-play returning an item to a store. (ADD, ADHD, BD, EBD, ED, ELL, LD, SLD, TBI)
- Provide reports from the BBB Web site for students to investigate. (ADD, ADHD, BD, EBD, ED, LD, OI, SLD, TBI)

Teaching Activity

6 Have each student complete Lesson VII—Consumer Fraud, Rights and Protection—of the Family Economics 101 program developed by the University of Wisconsin Cooperative Extension at www.uwex.edu/ces/flp/famecon/lesson7. Students will watch video clips, read short articles, and engage in various activities in the six-part lesson. Following the online experience, have each student write a summary of what he or she learned about fraud and consumer protection.

Accommodations/Modifications

- Have students work with a partner on the activities. (ASD, ELL, FAS, MR, TBI)
- Have students use assistive technology to access the Internet to complete the activities. (ADD, ADHD, BD, EBD, ED, HI, MR, OHI, OI, TBI, VI)
- Have students explain why it is important to know about consumer rights and protection. (ADD, ADHD, BD, EBD, ED, LD, SLD)
- Have students work at their own pace, and provide them with individual accommodations for the activities. (ADD, ADHD, ASD, BD, EBD, ED, ELL, FAS, HI, LD, MR, OHI, OI, SLD, TBI, VI)

Chapter 2 Activity Plan: Consumer Management Skills

Objective: To develop the skills necessary to manage personal and financial resources.

Teaching Activity

1 Have each student develop a time line for a short-term and a long-term goal. Students should select goals that are realistic yet challenging and that reflect their personal priorities and values. Students should include steps they will take to meet the goals and possible difficulties they may encounter along the way. They should identify individuals or groups they could draw support from in reaching their goals. Have volunteers share their goals and time line with the class. If possible, keep a record of the goals and return them to students at the completion of the course so they can see what they have accomplished.

Accommodations/Modifications

- Provide examples of short- and long-term goals students could use to develop their own ideas. (ADD, ADHD, BD, EBD, ED, LD, SLD)
- Provide a time line framework for students to use in developing their own goals. (ASD, ELL, FAS, MR, TBI)
- Have students work with a parent, teacher, or other adult to formulate appropriate goals. (ADD, ADHD, ASD, BD, EBD, ED, ELL, FAS, HI, LD, MR, OHI, OI, SLD, TBI, VI)
- Have students brainstorm a list of people or resources that could help individuals reach their short- and long-term goals. (ADD, ADHD, BD, EBD, ED, ELL, FAS, LD, MR, SLD, TBI)

Teaching Activity

2 Divide the class into six groups. Have each group research one type of resource available to consumers and share ideas for how the resource could be used to help meet short- and long-term goals. Students should also discuss possible opportunity costs associated with the resource and what could happen if the resource became scarce. Have students follow the guidelines in the textbook to share ideas on how to use the resource effectively. Have each group develop a ten-minute slide presentation on what was learned and present it to the class.

Accommodations/Modifications

- Provide a chart for students to record notes during the presentations. (ADD, ADHD, BD, EBD, ED, LD, SLD)
- Have students use assistive technology to complete the project. (ELL, HI, OHI, OI, VI)
- Invite a professional life coach to the classroom to explain how he or she helps clients reach their goals. Ask the coach to share some tips students might use in setting and achieving their own goals. (ADD, ADHD, BD, EBD, ED, LD, SLD, TBI)

Continued on next page

Teaching Activity

3 Have each student develop a plan to better manage time and energy spent at school, on homework, at a part-time job, in extracurricular activities, on household chores, and on other activities. Have students implement the steps of the management process and strategies for managing time and energy into their personal plan. Encourage students to take steps to implement the plan, reflect on their progress weekly, and make adjustments to their personal plan as necessary.

Accommodations/Modifications

- Have students make a detailed weekly schedule of their activities. (ADD, ADHD, BD, EBD, ED, LD, SLD)
- Have students develop a pie chart to show the breakdown of how they spend their time. (ADD, ADHD, BD, EBD, ED, LD, SLD)
- Have students make a list of activities they would consider time-wasters and evaluate how many are part of their own life. (ASD, ELL, FAS, MR, TBI)
- Provide students with a visual diagram of the management process that they can use to develop their plan. (ADD, ADHD, BD, EBD, ED, LD, SLD, TBI)

Teaching Activity

4 Have students explore factors that affect consumer decisions. Each student should select a major item that a family may need to purchase or fund, such as a house, car, or college education. Have students determine at least four factors that may impact the family's decision about the purchase. Students should explain how each factor might influence the decision the family makes. Have students share their ideas with the class.

Accommodations/Modifications

- Have students make a poster describing the process of making a decision about a major purchase. (ADD, ADHD, BD, EBD, ED, LD, SLD)
- Have students make a list of items a family may need to buy and locate pictures of the items in catalogs or store advertisements. (ASD, ELL, FAS, MR, TBI)
- Have students work with a partner for this activity. (ASD, ELL, FAS, MR, TBI)
- Have students locate information about the terms or duration of loans, mortgages, and student loans. (ADD, ADHD, BD, EBD, ED, LD, SLD)

Continued on next page

Teaching Activity

5 As a class, develop a rubric to evaluate sources of consumer information. The rubric should be designed broadly enough for use with a variety of media. After developing the rubric, have each student locate and evaluate four specific examples of consumer information from at least two different types of media. Students should use the rubric developed by the class, along with critical thinking skills, to evaluate the information and determine whether it is reliable. Have each student write a reflection on the importance of using reliable information for making consumer decisions.

Accommodations/Modifications

- Have students compare and contrast two or more advertisements from department or discount stores. (ASD, ELL, FAS, MR, TBI)
- Provide examples of criteria that could be included in the evaluation tool. (ADD, ADHD, BD, EBD, ED, LD, SLD)
- Have students make a checklist of necessary consumer information for selecting a particular item, such as a refrigerator, automobile, house, and so on. (ADD, ADHD, BD, EBD, ED, FAS, LD, SLD, TBI)
- Have students work with a partner for this activity. (ASD, ELL, FAS, MR, TBI)

Chapter 3 Activity Plan: Responsible Choices

Objective: To identify characteristics of responsible consumers and citizens.

Teaching Activity

1 Have students work in small groups to develop scenarios depicting ethical and honest consumer practices and scenarios depicting unethical or dishonest consumer behaviors. Have groups record short video clips illustrating the scenarios. After all the groups have recorded their video segments, have the class develop a study guide to accompany the video. Share the video and study guide with intermediate and middle-school teachers to use in their classrooms.

Accommodations/Modifications

- Develop scenarios and present them to students. Have them indicate whether the situation depicts ethical or unethical behavior. (ASD, ELL, FAS, MR, TBI)
- Allow students to use note cards or cue cards for the video production. (ADD, ADHD, BD, EBD, ED, ELL, LD, SLD)
- Have students develop a list of do's and don'ts for consumer shopping. (ASD, ELL, FAS, MR, TBI)
- Invite a consumer advocate to the classroom to discuss the responsibilities of being a consumer. (ADD, ADHD, BD, EBD, ED, LD, SLD, TBI)

Teaching Activity

2 Invite a community leader (superintendent, mayor, school board member, or city council member) to the classroom to discuss the responsibilities of being a citizen in a community. Ask the leader to share information about his or her leadership role in the community and how he or she works to instill values in the youth of the community. Ask the leader to provide examples of ways that young people can take an active role in their community.

Accommodations/Modifications

- Have students visit the office of the mayor or other public officials in the area. (ADD, ADHD, BD, EBD, ED, LD, MR, OHI, SLD)
- Have students use assistive technology or an interpreter for the presentation. (HI, VI)
- Provide students with a guided notes sheet for the presentation. (ADD, ADHD)
- Arrange for students to participate in a community clean-up day. (ADD, ADHD, ASD, BD, EBD, ED, ELL, FAS, HI, LD, MR, OHI, OI, SLD, TBI, VI)

Continued on next page

Teaching Activity

3 As a class, develop a list of twenty interview questions to ask local leaders. Have students work in pairs to arrange for an interview with a local leader. If possible, have the leaders come to the school during class time, and provide a quiet location for the interviews. Each student pair should prepare a ten-slide electronic presentation to inform the class about the leader they interviewed. Have each group make its presentation to the class and answer questions.

Accommodations/Modifications

- View a closed-captioned video about a famous leader. Discuss the person's leadership qualities. (ELL, HI, LD, OHI, OI, SLD, TBI)
- Have students use assistive technology (for instance, FM system, audio or video recorder) for the interview. (ADD, ADHD, ASD, ELL, FAS, HI, LD, MR, OHI, OI, SLD, TBI, VI)
- Have students read a book about the life of a famous leader. (ASD, HI, OHI, OI, SLD)
- Have students e-mail or write and send the questions for the interview. (ELL, HI, LD, OHI, OI, SLD, TBI)

Teaching Activity

4 Have students work in small groups to develop an educational program for young children about the dangers of chemicals. To assist in developing their program, students could use Internet resources, such as general poison safety information at http://www.wapc.org/safety.htm or poison prevention teaching aids at http://www.aapcc.org/teaching.htm. Arrange for students to present their program to young children.

Accommodations/Modifications

- View a closed-captioned video about household chemical safety. (ADD, ADHD, BD, EBD, ED, ELL, FAS, MR, TBI)
- Have students identify safety latches and products that can be used to secure chemicals in homes with young children. (ADD, ADHD, BD, EBD, ED, ELL, HI, LD, OHI, SLD, TBI)
- Have students work with a partner during this activity. (ASD, ELL, FAS, MR, TBI)
- Have students develop a video for parents on how to keep their children safe from chemicals in the home. (ADD, ADHD, LD, SLD)

Continued on next page

Teaching Activity

5 Have each student select an environmental topic from either the U.S. Environmental Protection Agency (http://www.epa.gov) or the U.S. government's Web site for Environment, Energy, and Agriculture (http://www.firstgov.gov/Citizen/Topics/Environment_Agriculture.shtml). Each student should research the selected environmental concern or issue; identify the major factors affecting the topic; identify federal, state, and local governments' roles related to the topic; and identify the roles and responsibilities of consumers relative to the topic. Each student should prepare a poster to increase awareness of the issue or concern and to educate others about what they can do to help. Have students share the posters in class and display them in the school for others to view.

Accommodations/Modifications

- Have students work with a partner for this activity. (ASD, ELL, FAS, MR, TBI)
- Arrange for students to participate in a community clean-up day. (ADD, ADHD, ASD, BD, EBD, ED, ELL, FAS, HI, LD, MR, OHI, OI, SLD, TBI, VI)
- Invite a speaker from a natural resources agency to discuss ways consumers can help improve the environment. (ADD, ADHD, BD, EBD, ED, ELL, FAS, HI, LD, MR, OHI, OI, SLD, TBI, VI)
- Have students teach a lesson on environmental concerns to young children. (ADD, ADHD, BD, EBD, ED, LD, SLD)

Chapter 4 Activity Plan: Career Decisions

Objective: To combine knowledge of careers with personal interests to determine potential career paths.

Teaching Activity

1 Invite a panel of adults to the classroom to discuss how they balance multiple roles, such as parent, spouse, employee, and community member. Ensure that there is a variety of individuals, such as those without children, parents of young children, parents of teens, single parents, and retired adults. Have the class develop a list of questions for the panel members prior to the event and share the questions with the guests in advance. After the panel presentation, have each student write a reflection on strategies they could use in the future to balance work, family, career, and community roles.

Accommodations/Modifications

- Provide students with copies of the questions so they can record responses from the panel members. (ADD, ADHD, BD, EBD, ED, LD, SLD, TBI)
- Have students cut out pictures of families with adults who work outside the home. (ASD, FAS, MR, TBI)
- Have students interview a working parent. (ADD, ADHD, BD, EBD, ED, LD, SLD)
- Have students list difficulties that working families may encounter. (ADD, ADHD, LD, SLD)

Teaching Activity

2 Work with the guidance staff at the school or a local career counseling service to arrange for each student to complete a career interest and skills inventory to identify jobs or career areas the student may be interested in pursuing. After analyzing the results, each student should arrange to job-shadow someone in a career or job that is of interest to the student. Prior to the job-shadow experience, each student should research the job or career field of interest. Following the job-shadow experience, have each student present information to the class about the career area he or she is interested in, details about the career area from research, and what was learned from the job-shadow experience.

Accommodations/Modifications

- Find interest surveys students can complete on the computer. (ADD, ADHD, BD, EBD, ED, LD, SLD, TBI)
- Have a partner read the survey aloud to a student. (ASD, ELL, FAS, MR, TBI)
- Have students develop materials related to their job-shadow experience to place in their transition portfolio. (ASD, FAS, HI, LD, MR, SLB, TBI, VI)
- Have students visit a career center in the area, such as the Department of Workforce Development or Division of Vocational Rehabilitation. (ADD, ADHD, ASD, BD, EBD, ED, ELL, FAS, HI, LD, MR, OHI, OI, SLD, TBI, VI)

Continued on next page

Teaching Activity

3 Have students work with a partner to research educational opportunities in their community or regional area. Have each pair identify a school, a training center, or other educational option and research the types of programs, certifications, and degrees that are offered; estimated tuition; types of classes offered; and information on recent graduates. Have students share the information with the class.

Accommodations/Modifications

- Have students tour a postsecondary education campus in the area. (ADD, ADHD, BD, EBD, ED, ELL, HI, LD, OHI, OI, SLD, TBI, VI)
- Invite a guidance counselor to the classroom to discuss the application procedures for postsecondary education and required tests for acceptance. (ADD, ADHD, BD, EBD, ED, ELL, HI, LD, OHI, OI, SLD, TBI, VI)
- Locate examples of postsecondary education application forms. Have students practice completing the forms. (ADD, ADHD, ELL, FAS, LD, MR, OHI, OI, SLD, TBI)
- Have students find out what services postsecondary education institutions offer for students with special learning needs. (ADD, ADHD, ASD, BD, EBD, ED, ELL, FAS, HI, LD, MR, OHI, OI, SLD, TBI, VI)

Teaching Activity

4 Have each student use several different resources to locate four potential job openings the student would be interested in applying for. Using the information they locate, students should write up the duties of each job, any education or special training required, necessary materials or information for application, and any other information available through the job posting or from the potential employer.

Accommodations/Modifications

- Have students define the abbreviations used in job advertisements. (ADD, ADHD, ASD, BD, EBD, ED, ELL, FAS, LD, MR, OHI, OI, SLD, TBI)
- Have students identify jobs they would like to do and jobs they would not like to do. (ADD, ADHD, ASD, BD, EBD, ED, MR)
- Enlarge the sample application forms for students to complete. (ASD, FAS, MR, TBI)
- Locate online or computerized application forms. (ADD, ADHD, BD, EBD, ED, ELL, FAS, LD, OHI, OI, TBI)

Continued on next page

Teaching Activity

5 Divide the class into ten groups. Have each group prepare two video segments about behavior on the job—one segment about appropriate workplace behavior and another about inappropriate behavior. Title the video "Ten Ways to Keep Your Job and Ten Ways to Lose It." Play the entire video for the class. If possible, share the video with other classes that study employability skills and workplace behaviors.

Accommodations/Modifications

- Allow students to use notes or cue cards during the video production. (ASD, ELL, FAS, MR, TBI)
- Have students list appropriate and inappropriate workplace behaviors. (ADD, ADHD, ASD, BD, EBD, ED, FAS, MR, TBI)
- Interview an employer about the expectations he or she has of employees. (ADD, ADHD, BD, EBD, ED, LD, SLD, TBI)
- View a closed-captioned video about workplace skills. (ADD, ADHD, BD, EBD, ED, ELL, FAS, HI, LD, MR, OHI, OI, SLD, TBI)

Chapter 5 Activity Plan: The U.S. Economic System

Objective: To explain the roles of producer, consumer, and government in the U.S. economy.

Teaching Activity

1 Divide the class into four groups. Have each group become experts on one type of economic system. Each group should use the textbook and other print and online resources to investigate the chosen economic system. Groups should prepare a slide presentation for the class that defines and explains the economic system, identifies where the system is used, and provides detailed examples of how the system operates.

Accommodations/Modifications

- Have students work with a partner for this activity. (ASD, ELL, FAS, MR, TBI)
- Provide guiding questions for students' research. (ADD, ADHD, BD, EBD, ED, LD, SLD)
- Develop a chart for students to record notes about each economic system during the presentations. (ADD, ADHD, BD, EBD, ED, LD, SLD, TBI)
- Have students role-play people living in the different types of economic systems. (ADD, ADHD, LD, SLD)

Teaching Activity

2 Have each student complete the interactive online Exploration in Economics lessons on supply and demand from the University of Omaha at http://ecedweb.unomaha.edu/Dem_Sup/demand.htm. At the end of each lesson, lead the class in a discussion to answer the questions listed. At the completion of all the lessons, students will have the opportunity to perform an interactive self-quiz to measure their understanding of supply and demand concepts.

Accommodations/Modifications

- Have students work with a partner for the lessons. (ASD, ELL, MR, TBI)
- Use a projector to lead the students through the lessons. (ASD, BD, EBD, ED, ELL, FAS, LD, MR, OHI, OI, SLD, TBI)
- Have students develop a poster or other visual describing the principles of supply and demand in their own words, using products and/or services they are familiar with. (ADD, ADHD, BD, EBD, ED, LD, SLD, TBI)
- Provide students with key questions from each lesson to assist them in reviewing for the end quiz. (ADD, ADHD, BD, EBD, ED, LD, SLD)

Continued on next page

Teaching Activity

3 Have students find examples of ways stores and companies compete for consumer business. Students could use magazines, flyers, coupons, promotional materials, store policies, television or radio advertisements, and billboards as evidence of competition among businesses. Have students share the examples they find. Then have students discuss how they, their families, and society in general benefit from competition. Encourage students to share examples of how they can use their consumer power to influence the economy.

Accommodations/Modifications

- Have students list some benefits and drawbacks of competition in business. (ADD, ADHD, BD, EBD, ED, LD, SLD)
- Have students visit stores to identify policies or in-store promotions that acknowledge competition among stores. (ADD, ADHD, BD, EBD, ED, ELL, LD, SLD)
- Have students look at advertisements from several different stores to compare similar products. (ASD, ELL, FAS, MR, TBI)
- Have students make a list of reasons they may choose to shop at one store instead of another. (ASD, ELL, FAS, MR, TBI)

Teaching Activity

4 Have students work in small groups to research and present information regarding programs and services that federal, state, and local governments provide for U.S. citizens. Students may use the resource ideas found in the textbook and locate additional ideas and resources at the U.S. government's Web site at http://first.gov/. Have groups share information about the programs or services they researched and explain how individuals, families, communities, and society in general benefit from these programs or services.

Accommodations/Modifications

- Have students identify the types of programs and services provided by local, county, state, and federal governments. (ADD, ADHD, ASD, BD, EBD, ED, ELL, LD, SLD, TBI)
- Invite a local policymaker to the classroom to discuss the programs and services provided by the government. (ADD, ADHD, BD, EBD, ED, ELL, LD, SLD, TBI)
- Have students locate recent newspaper or magazine articles related to government programs or services in their community. (BD, EBD, ED, LD, SLD)
- Have students interview members of the school board to find out how they budget money and determine school spending. (ADD, ADHD, BD, EBD, ED, LD, SLD)

Continued on next page

Teaching Activity

5 Invite the directors or coordinators from several local public assistance programs to be a part of a panel discussion in the classroom. Have program representatives share information regarding the goods and services they provide to individuals, families, and communities in need. Encourage representatives to distribute printed materials or pamphlets to the class for the students to learn more about the services offered by each group. Encourage students to ask questions of the panel members. Following the presentation, students may be interested in performing a service-learning activity to benefit a local public assistance program. Have students brainstorm ideas and decide on a project they feel will be the most beneficial.

Accommodations/Modifications

- ◆ Have students visit several of these community programs to learn about their services. (ADD, ADHD, ASD, BD, EBD, ED, ELL, FAS, HI, LD, MR, OHI, OI, SLD, TBI, VI)
- ◆ Have students take notes during the presentation to use in a follow-up discussion. (ADD, ADHD, BD, EBD, ED, LD, SLD)
- ◆ View a closed-captioned video about programs in the state, county, or community that serve individuals and families in need. (ADD, ADHD, BD, EBD, ED, ELL, FAS, HI, LD, MR, OHI, OI, SLD, TBI)
- ◆ Have students develop a resource inventory of services in their community. (ADD, ADHD, BD, EBD, ED, LD, SLD, TBI)

Chapter 6 Activity Plan: The Health of the Economy

Objective: To draw conclusions about the economy by analyzing economic indicators.

Teaching Activity

1 Have each student research a factor (past or present) that has impacted the U.S. economy. Students might select general factors, such as war, or specific factors, such as the invention of the cotton gin, airplane, or online commerce. Have each student use the Internet and two or three other sources to locate information about the topic. Have each student present the information to the class, using at least two visual aids to demonstrate the impact of the topic on the economy. Following each presentation, have students write a short reflection about the impact that the factor has had or continues to have on the economy.

Accommodations/Modifications

- Provide students with a specific topic and resource ideas. (ADD, ADHD, BD, EBD, ED, LD, SLD, TBI)
- Provide scenarios or examples for students and have them describe how the situation positively and/or negatively affects the economy. (ASD, BD, EBD, ED, ELL, HI, LD, OHI, OI, SLD, TBI, VI)
- Have students work with a partner for this activity. (ASD, ELL, FAS, MR, SLD)
- Have students use assistive technology and/or presentation software to research and present their information to the class. (ADD, ADHD, BD, EBD, ED, HI, LD, OHI, OI, SLD, TBI, VI)

Teaching Activity

2 Have students work with a partner to explore one of the economic indicators used to measure the economy's performance over time. Students could select topics from and use resources found at the U.S. Census Bureau's Web site at http://www.census.gov/cgi-bin/briefroom/BriefRm. Students should research their topic and share an overview of the main points with the class. As students work, have them keep a list of unfamiliar words and definitions.

Accommodations/Modifications

- Have students graph trends in the U.S. economy over a period of time. (ADD, ADHD, LD, SLD)
- Invite a social studies or an economics teacher to the class to discuss indicators used to measure the health of the economy. (ADD, ADHD, BD, EBD, ED, LD, SLD)
- Provide students with scenarios and have them determine whether they indicate economic growth or decline. (ADD, ADHD, BD, EBD, ED, LD, SLD, TBI)
- Have students locate recent newspaper or magazine articles related to economic indicators. (BD, EBD, ED, LD, SLD)

Continued on next page

Teaching Activity

3 Use the Role of Government: The National Debt vs. The Deficit lesson at http://www.econedlink.org to have students explore the national debt, federal budget deficit, and related information. Students can get a visual description of the federal budget spending at http://www.federalbudget.com/. The class may also be interested in using the national debt clock at http://www.brillig.com/debt_clock to track the national debt for a day, a week, or longer. Keep a running record of the national debt posted in the classroom.

Accommodations/Modifications

- Have students work with a partner on the lesson. (ASD, ELL, FAS, MR, TBI)
- Have students identify the types of things that local, county, state, and federal governments spend money on. (ADD, ADHD, ASD, BD, EBD, ED, ELL, LD, SLD, TBI)
- Invite a local policymaker to the classroom to discuss how the government spends money. (ADD, ADHD, BD, EBD, ED, ELL, LD, SLD, TBI)
- Have students locate recent newspaper or magazine articles related to government spending, budgets, or the national debt. (BD, EBD, ED, LD, SLD)

Teaching Activity

4 Invite a representative from a local bank or credit union to the classroom to discuss the Federal Reserve System and the money supply. Have the representative discuss how decisions made at the federal level impact business and consumer decisions. The representative may be able to share information on current interest rates and other figures, such as APR and APY. Invite students to ask questions of the representative. Following the presentation, have each student write a one-page summary of the information they learned from the speaker and how it relates to the chapter information.

Accommodations/Modifications

- View a closed-captioned video on the Federal Reserve System. (ADD, ADHD, BD, EBD, ED, HI, LD, MR, OHI, OI, SLD, TBI)
- Have students identify current APR and APY from local financial institutions. (ADD, ADHD, BD, EBD, ED, LD, SLD)
- Have students record information during the presentation to assist in developing a summary. (ADD, ADHD, BD, EBD, ED, LD, SLD, TBI)
- Have students use the Internet to locate information on the Federal Reserve System. (ADD, ADHD)

Continued on next page

Teaching Activity

5 Have each student develop a three-dimensional model of the business cycle. Students should label and define each stage. Students should also explain factors that may influence the ups and downs of the cycle and the consequences these fluctuations may have on businesses and consumers. Have each student describe his or her model to the class and explain the factors that may influence businesses and consumers. Display the business cycle models in the school library or other public viewing area.

Accommodations/Modifications

- Have students work with a partner to develop the model. (ASD, ELL, FAS, MR, TBI)
- Provide students with an example of a model. (ADD, ADHD, BD, EBD, ED, LD, SLD)
- Visit local businesses to learn about the cycles they experience in their business. (ADD, ADHD, BD, EBD, ED, LD, SLD)
- Create scenarios for students that illustrate factors that may influence business cycles. (ADD, ADHD, BD, EBD, ED, LD, SLD)

Chapter 7 Activity Plan: Global Economics

Objective: To study policies, restrictions, and agreements concerning international economics.

Teaching Activity

1 Have students find newspaper articles on global issues, such as imports and exports, sourcing and offshore production, laws and regulations, trade agreements, and international laws pertaining to business. Have students form small groups to discuss the articles and the issues making news. Following the discussions, have each student write a one-page summary describing the issues he or she learned about.

Accommodations/Modifications

- ◆ Provide the newspaper articles for students. (ADD, ADHD, BD, EBD, ED)
- ◆ Have students use the Internet to locate articles. (ADD, ADHD, LD, SLD)
- ◆ Have students use assistive technology for this activity. (OHI, OI, TBI, VI)
- ◆ Highlight the articles. (ELL, LD, SLD)

Teaching Activity

2 Have each student learn about an organization that promotes fair wages and fair trade for low-income artisans and farmers from around the world. Have students examine the Web site of each organization and report their findings to the rest of class. Some organizations are listed here.

- Worldly Goods: www.worldlygoods.org
- Ten Thousand Villages®: www.tenthousandvillages.com
- International Federation of Alternative Trade: www.ifat.org
- The Fair Trade Federation: http://fairtradefederation.org
- SERRV International: www.agreatergift.org

Following the activity, have students brainstorm the benefits of these organizations.

Accommodations/Modifications

- ◆ Visit an international artisan shop with students. (ADD, ADHD, BD, EBD, ED, ELL, LD, MR, OHI, OI, SLD, TBI, VI)
- ◆ Have students learn about the artisans that sell their goods on the Web sites. (ASD, MR)
- ◆ Have students use assistive technology for this activity. (HI, OHI, OI, TBI, VI)
- ◆ Have students learn about an organization in their community that provides goods or services to needy people in other countries. (ADD, ADHD, BD, EBD, ED, ELL, MR)

Continued on next page

Teaching Activity

3 Divide the class into two groups. Have one group investigate imports, or products that are brought into the U.S. from other countries, and the other group investigate exports, or products the U.S. sends to other countries. Once each group has identified several import or export products, have each student select one specific product to research. Have each student develop three to five electronic slides describing the product and the role it plays in the balance of trade. Have the students in each group compile their individual slides into one presentation and present the information to the rest of the class.

Accommodations/Modifications

- Provide a list of products for students to select from. (ASD, ELL, FAS, MR)
- Develop a combined list of imports and exports and have students sort them by category. (ADD, ADHD, BD, EBD, ED, LD, SLD)
- Have students select a country and learn about its products. (ADD, ADHD, BD, EBD, ED, LD, SLD)
- Have students use assistive technology for this activity. (HI, OHI, OI, TBI, VI)

Teaching Activity

4 Have students use online currency converter tools to compare the value of the U.S. dollar to currency in other countries. Students may be interested in locating exchange rate information for countries where they have traveled or for countries where they may wish to travel. Have each student perform at least ten online conversions. Following this activity, have students write a short reflection on how this information could be useful.

Accommodations/Modifications

- Have students visit a financial institution to learn about currency exchange. (ADD, ADHD, BD, EBD, ED, ELL, LD, SLD)
- Have students use a world map to identify countries and their currency. (ADD, ADHD, ASD, ELL, LD, MR, SLD, TBI)
- Have a world language teacher speak to the class about how products are purchased in another country and what items would cost in U.S. dollars. (ADD, ADHD, ASD, BD, EBD, ED, ELL, FAS, HI, LD, MR, OHI, OI, SLD, TBI, VI)
- Have students work with a partner to perform the online activity. (ASD, ELL, FAS, MR)

Continued on next page

Teaching Activity

5 Divide the class into two groups for a class debate about protectionism versus fair trade. Have students use the textbook, magazines, and the Internet to develop an understanding of and support for their side of the issue. Following the debate, have each student write a reflection on his or her position on protectionism and fair trade, including reasons for the position taken.

Accommodations/Modifications

- Have students use note cards during the debate. (ADD, ADHD, BD, EBD, ED, LD, SLD, TBI)
- Have students work with a partner to research and present their views. (ASD, ELL, FAS, MR, TBI)
- Provide students with highlighted resources for their research. (ADD, ADHD, BD, EBD, ED, ELL, LD, SLD, TBI)
- Invite a social studies or economics teacher to the classroom to discuss fair trade. (ADD, ADHD, BD, EBD, ED, ELL, LD, MR, SLD, TBI, VI)

Chapter 8 Activity Plan: Income and Taxes

Objective: To interpret information about income and tax preparation.

Teaching Activity

1 Have each student use classified newspaper advertisements and online job search engines to find two openings for full-time, part-time, temporary, and contract employment. Students should then locate two examples of each of the following types of jobs: those that pay a salary, pay an hourly wage, pay by the piece (piecework), pay on commission, offer bonuses, and let workers earn tips. As a class, discuss the type of jobs identified for each employment classification and type of pay.

Accommodations/Modifications

- Develop a chart for students to use to record the information. (ADD, ADHD, BD, EBD, ED, LD, MR, SLD, TBI)
- Have students determine the approximate weekly, biweekly, monthly, and annual income for full-time hourly wage positions. (ADD, ADHD, BD, EBD, ED, ELL, FAS, LD, SLD, TBI)
- Have students locate a part-time job they would be interested in. Have them identify the wage per hour and how many hours per week they might work if they had this job. Have students determine what their income per week would be. (ADD, ADHD, ASD, BD, EBD, ED, ELL, LD, MR, OHI, OI, SLD, TBI)
- Have the class discuss the benefits and drawbacks of the various types of pay they researched. (ADD, ADHD, ASD, BD, EBD, ED, ELL, FAS, HI, LD, MR, OHI, OI, SLD, TBI, VI)

Teaching Activity

2 Invite a human resources manager to the classroom to discuss the types of benefits employers may offer to employees, including insurance, retirement, vacation, holidays, sick leave, and so on. Have the manager describe the choices employees might have for their benefits and explain that many employees must pay a portion of their benefit premiums. Encourage students to ask questions of the speaker. Following the presentation, have each student write a summary of the information he or she learned about the types of benefits often associated with employment.

Accommodations/Modifications

- Have students record notes during the presentation to use in developing their summary. (ADD, ADHD, LD, SLD, TBI)
- Locate pamphlets or brochures that describe employee benefits for students to view. (ADD, ADHD, BD, EBD, ED, ELL, LD, SLD, TBI)
- Have students look at job advertisements to identify whether or not they include benefits. (ASD, ELL, FAS, MR, TBI)
- Have students compare the costs of employer-sponsored benefits with direct payment of benefit services. (BD, EBD, ED, LD, SLD, TBI)

Continued on next page

Teaching Activity

3 Use module 1 of the Making Choices About Jobs program at http://www.otan.us/webfarm/laes/modules/mod1/m01plan.html to have students identify the types of deductions from a paycheck and calculate several scenarios for earnings based on hours worked, net pay, deductions, withholdings, and so on.

Accommodations/Modifications

- Have students review sample paycheck summary statements to identify types of deductions and withholdings. (ADD, ADHD, BD, EBD, ED, LD, SLD)
- Highlight the paycheck summary statements and provide full descriptions of the abbreviations used. (ELL, FAS, MR)
- Have students complete sample W-9 and other tax-related employment forms. (ADD, ADHD, ASD, ELL, FAS, LD, MR, SLD, TBI)
- Have students identify and describe the types of paycheck deductions, withholdings, and taxes. (ADD, ADHD, BD, EBD, ED, LD)

Teaching Activity

4 Invite a Certified Public Accountant or tax professional to the classroom to explain how to prepare for and file taxes annually. Have the guest review the key terms associated with paying income taxes and help students understand their responsibility for taxes. Following the presentation, have each student record what he or she learned from the presentation about preparing, filing, and paying income taxes.

Accommodations/Modifications

- Have students record notes during the presentation to use in developing the summary. (ADD, ADHD, LD, SLD, TBI)
- Prior to the speaker's visit, provide students with terms and definitions associated with tax preparation. (ADD, ADHD, BD, EBD, ED, ELL, FAS, LD, MR, SLD, TBI)
- Visit a tax preparer's office with students to learn about the documents needed for tax preparation. (ADD, ADHD, BD, EBD, ED, ELL, FAS, HI, LD, OHI, OI, SLD, TBI)
- Have students make a list of the many ways tax dollars are spent. (ADD, ADHD, BD, EBD, ED, LD, SLD)

Continued on next page

Teaching Activity

5 Have students use online tax preparation services, such as Turbo Tax at http://www.turbotax.com, to practice completing their own tax return. Ask students to bring the necessary documents to class or provide their best estimate of the information needed to file a tax return.

Accommodations/Modifications

- Provide sample tax forms for students to complete. (ADD, ADHD, LD, SLD, TBI)
- Locate resources for individuals with disabilities to use for tax preparation. (HI, OHI, OI, VI)
- Have students locate tax preparation assistance on the Internet. (ADD, ADHD, LD, SLD)

Chapter 9 Activity Plan: Financial Planning

Objective: To summarize financial planning strategies and methods.

Teaching Activity

1 Have students brainstorm examples of assets and liabilities that individuals and families may have. Record all the ideas on the board. Have each student prepare a balance sheet of his or her own estimated assets and liabilities and then determine his or her approximate net worth. Have each student develop a balance sheet for expected assets, liabilities, and net worth in 10, 15, or 20 years. Have students provide reasoning for their calculations.

Accommodations/Modifications

- Provide students with examples of assets and liabilities and have them sort the examples by category. (ASD, ELL, FAS, MR, TBI)
- Have students develop a poster describing the differences between assets and liabilities. (ADD, ADHD, BD, EBD, ED, LD, SLD)
- Provide students with a worksheet to use in forecasting their assets, liabilities, and net worth. (ADD, ADHD, BD, EBD, ED, ELL, LD, SLD, TBI)
- Provide a variety of financial scenarios and have students calculate the individuals' net worth. (ADD, ADHD, BD, EBD, ED, LD)

Teaching Activity

2 As a class, develop a list of financial management and planning questions to ask adults who are in one of the family life stages discussed in the chapter. Have each student interview an adult family member or an adult he or she knows well about how changes in the family, such as marriage, parenthood, children moving out, and aging or retirement, have impacted the person's financial management or planning. Have students discuss the interview responses in class.

Accommodations/Modifications

- Have students make a poster describing family life changes. (ASD, ELL, FAS, MR, TBI)
- Provide students with scenarios that describe family life changes and have them predict how the situation may impact financial management. (ADD, ADHD, ASD, EBD, ED, LD, SLD)
- Have students brainstorm a list of expenses associated with parenting. (ADD, ADHD, ASD, BD, EBD, ED, ELL, FAS, HI, LD, MR, OHI, OI, SLD, TBI, VI)
- Have students make a timeline showing the family life cycle and list financial considerations specific to each stage. (ADD, ADHD, BD, EBD, ED, ELL, FAS, LD, SLD, TBI)

Continued on next page

Teaching Activity

3 Have students use financial software or a financial software simulation to perform financial functions a family would generally perform in a typical month. If possible, have students use more than one type of software to compare and contrast the programs' features and ease of use.

Accommodations/Modifications

- Provide a chart for students to use in performing the comparisons. (ADD, ADHD, BD, EBD, ED, LD, SLD)
- Have students use assistive technology for this activity. (ASD, HI, OHI, OI, VI)
- Have students compare and contrast doing financial functions with a software program and by hand. (BD, EBD, ED, LD, SLD)
- Have students list the benefits and drawbacks of using financial software. (ADD, ADHD, BD, EBD, ED, LD, SLD)

Teaching Activity

4 Have each student develop an outline to use, both now and in the future, to organize important records and documents. Students should use information from the chapter as well as from parents and other sources to determine which documents and items to include in the outline. Students should also note the amount of time different types of documents should be kept. Have students prepare a short written report about the organization of their personal and financial records and the importance of keeping them organized.

Accommodations/Modifications

- Provide students with a general outline for this activity and have them list specific documents in each area. (ADD, ADHD, BD, EBD, ED, ELL, LD, SLD, TBI)
- Have students visit a bank or financial institution to learn about lock boxes and safe document storage. (ADD, ADHD, BD, EBD, ED, ELL, LD, SLD, TBI)
- Have students create a file box to use in the future. Students should apply the organization system developed in this activity to arrange the file system. (ADD, ADHD, BD, EBD, ED, LD, SLD, TBI)
- Have students make a list of important documents to keep and/or photocopy. (ASD, ELL, FAS, MR, TBI)

Continued on next page

Teaching Activity

5 Have students visit the U.S. Financial Literacy and Education Commission's Web site at http://www.mymoney.gov to select and investigate a topic on budgeting and financial planning. Have students offer five- to ten-minute informational seminars on their topic to the rest of the class. Students should prepare an outline of the points they wish to cover and have handouts of important information to share with the class.

Accommodations/Modifications

- Have students work with a partner or in a small group for this activity. (ASD, ELL, FAS, MR, TBI)
- Provide resources for students to use for reporting on their topic. (ADD, ADHD, BD, EBD, ED, LD, SLD)
- Provide guiding questions for students' investigation. (ADD, ADHD, BD, EBD, ED, LD, SLD, TBI)
- Have students use presentation software to develop and deliver their presentation. (ADD, ADHD, BD, EBD, ED, LD, SLD)

Chapter 10 Activity Plan: Banking

Objective: To analyze and explain banking services available to consumers.

Teaching Activity

1 Divide the class into four groups. Have each group research one type of financial institution, the services it offers to customers, and up-to-date information from local financial institutions of the type being researched. Have each group present its information to the class. Make a large chart comparing the types of financial institutions to display in the classroom.

Accommodations/Modifications

- Prepare a chart for students to use when gathering their information. (ADD, ADHD, BD, EBD, ED, LD, SLD, TBI)
- Have students use an overhead projector to show their findings. (ASD, ELL, FAS, MR, TBI, VI)
- Have students use the Internet, telephone books, and other resources to gather the information. (ADD, ADHD, BD, EBD, ED, ELL, FAS, HI, LD, MR, SLD, TBI)
- Have students use assistive technology, such as speakerphones and TTY systems, to communicate with local financial institutions. (ASD, ELL, FAS, HI, MR, OHI, OI, VI)

Teaching Activity

2 Invite a representative from a local bank to discuss the electronic banking services available for individuals and businesses. Have students prepare questions for the speaker in advance. Provide the guest with the students' questions prior to the presentation. Have the speaker include information about the benefits and drawbacks of electronic banking services. Following the presentation, have each student write a short reflection on his or her views of electronic banking.

Accommodations/Modifications

- Have students locate articles in newspapers or magazines about electronic banking methods. (LD, SLD)
- Use a projector to demonstrate electronic banking transactions. (ADD, ADHD, ASD, BD, EBD, ED, ELL, FAS, HI, LD, MR, OHI, OI, SLD, TBI)
- Have students list the benefits and drawbacks of using electronic banking services. (ADD, ADHD, BD, EBD, ED, LD, SLD)
- Have students record notes during the presentation to use in their reflection. (ADD, ADHD, LD, SLD, TBI)

Continued on next page

Teaching Activity

3 Use resources from Money Instructor at http://www.moneyinstructor.com/checks.asp to have students manage a personal checking account. Students should learn to write checks, enter transactions in a checkbook register, balance a checkbook register, perform monthly checkbook reconciliation, learn the purpose of check endorsement, and practice completing checking account deposit slips. Have students complete the interactive lessons on the Web site, and provide additional lessons with the resources provided.

Accommodations/Modifications

- Enlarge or highlight lesson materials. (ASD, ELL, FAS, MR, TBI, VI)
- Provide students with the word versions of any number amounts needed. (ASD, ELL, FAS, LD, MR, SLD, TBI)
- Have students visit a bank to learn about forms and documents associated with various types of accounts. (ADD, ADHD, ASD, BD, EBD, ED, ELL, FAS, HI, LD, MR, OHI, OI, SLD, TBI)
- Have students use personal budgeting software to perform financial recordkeeping tasks. (ADD, ADHD, LD, SLD, TBI)

Teaching Activity

4 Divide the class into seven small groups. Have each group find additional information on one of the alternative payment methods identified in Section 10.4 of the textbook. Students may use the Internet or contact financial institutions to learn more about these payment methods. Have each group share information with the rest of the class about the method and why a person might choose to use that option.

Accommodations/Modifications

- Have students make a chart to describe the benefits and drawbacks of each payment method. (ADD, ADHD, BD, EBD, ED, LD, SLD, TBI)
- Have students work with a partner for this activity. (ASD, ELL, FAS, MR, TBI)
- Visit a financial institution with students to learn more about various payment methods. (ADD, ADHD, BD, EBD, ED, ELL, LD, SLD, TBI)
- Have students identify store policies related to types of payment accepted. (ADD, ADHD, BD, EBD, ED, ELL, LD, SLD)

Continued on next page

Teaching Activity

5 Have each student make a list of personal criteria for selecting a financial institution, including the student's needs and preferences for services. Then have the class research banks, credit unions, and savings and loans institutions in the community to determine the best financial institution for their personal needs. Students may gather information from the institutions' Web sites or directly from the institutions. Have each student compare and contrast a minimum of three financial institutions and choose one that would best meet his or her needs. Have students provide justification for their selection.

Accommodations/Modifications

- Visit two or more financial institutions with students to compare the services offered. (ADD, ADHD, BD, EBD, ED, ELL, HI, LD, OHI, OI, SLD, TBI, VI)
- Provide students with a chart to record information about each financial institution they research. (ADD, ADHD, BD, EBD, ED, LD, SLD)
- Have students research two financial institutions rather than three. (ASD, ELL, FAS, MR, SLD, TBI)
- Have students gather brochures or pamphlets from various financial institutions to compare and contrast the services offered. (ADD, ADHD, BD, EBD, ED, ELL, LD, SLD)

Chapter 11 Activity Plan: Consumer Credit

Objective: To learn to manage credit in a responsible manner.

Teaching Activity

1 Use the unit on credit from the Family Economics and Financial Education program from Montana State University at http://www.familyfinance.montana.edu/curriculum.php?categoryID=6 to help students define and understand credit, select and manage credit cards effectively, and understand information in a credit report. Teachers may be prompted to create a profile to access this program.

Accommodations/Modifications

- Have students work with a partner on the unit activities. (ASD, ELL, FAS, MR, TBI)
- Have students use assistive technology to complete the activities. (ADD, ADHD, BD, EBD, ED, HI, MR, OHI, OI, TBI, VI)
- Have students identify why it is important to have good credit. (ADD, ADHD, BD, EBD, ED, LD, SLD)
- Have students work at their own pace and use individual accommodations for the unit activities. (ADD, ADHD, ASD, BD, EBD, ED, ELL, FAS, HI, LD, MR, OHI, OI, SLD, TBI, VI)

Teaching Activity

2 Have students work in groups of three or four to develop twenty "if, then" statements about credit. Ten of the statements should emphasize positive consequences of using credit, and ten statements should emphasize negative consequences of using credit. Have students write the "if" portion of the statement on one side of an index card and the corresponding "then" statement on the reverse side. Students in a group should work together to ensure the accuracy of each statement. Then rotate the cards among groups. Each group should read the "if" statements and predict the "then" statements. Continue until each group has had an opportunity to read each card.

Accommodations/Modifications

- Provide examples of "if, then" statements for students to follow. (ADD, ADHD, BD, EBD, ED, LD, SLD)
- Provide the "if" portion of the statements and have students complete the "then" portion. (ASD, ELL, FAS, MR, TBI)
- Have students work with a partner during this activity. (ASD, ELL, FAS, MR, TBI)
- Provide scenarios for students to use when developing the statements. (ADD, ADHD, BD, EBD, ED, LD, SLD)

Continued on next page

Teaching Activity

3 Have each student visit one of the three national credit reporting agencies' Web sites to learn about credit, credit reports, credit history, credit scores, and credit rights. Have students engage in a think-pair-share session to teach others what they learned. Have students develop a chart to record the pertinent information.

Accommodations/Modifications

- ◆ Have students use assistive technology for this activity. (HI, OHI, OI, VI)
- ◆ Develop a list of vocabulary terms for the chapter and have students locate the definitions. (ELL, FAS, LD, SLD, TBI)
- ◆ Provide students with a chart to record information during the sharing session. (ADD, ADHD, BD, EBD, ED, LD, SLD)
- ◆ Locate an example of a credit report. Have students identify the symbols and indicators used on the report. (ADD, ADHD, LD, SLD)

Teaching Activity

4 Have students gather credit card promotions for both private label and general purpose cards through mailings, magazines, or pamphlets. Have each student select three cards to compare and contrast, using the credit card terms in the textbook. Students should share their analysis with the class.

Accommodations/Modifications

- ◆ Provide a chart for students to record information about the cards they are researching. (ADD, ADHD, BD, EBD, ED, LD, SLD, TBI)
- ◆ Enlarge or highlight credit card terms and restriction information. (ASD, ELL, FAS, LD, MR, SLD, TBI, VI)
- ◆ As a class, develop a wall chart of students' findings. (ADD, ADHD, BD, EBD, ED, ELL, LD, SLD, TBI)
- ◆ Have students work with a partner to research and present their information. (ASD, ELL, FAS, MR, TBI)

Continued on next page

Teaching Activity

5 Have a loan officer from a bank or other financial institution visit the classroom to share information about loans. Have the guest review basic loan terms with the class and describe the types of loans available. Have the loan professional describe the terms and conditions of several types of loans and how individuals may qualify and apply for such loans. If possible, have the guest share a copy of a loan application with the students or describe the typical process of applying for a loan. Following the presentation, have each student name and describe one type of loan he or she may need at some point, and discuss information learned about this type of loan.

Accommodations/Modifications

- Obtain sample loan forms to have students complete. (ADD, ADHD, BD, EBD, ED, ELL, FAS, LD, OHI, OI, SLD, TBI)
- Have students make a poster of purchases that may require a loan. (ASD, ELL, FAS, MR, TBI)
- Have students list the benefits and drawbacks of loans. (ADD, ADHD, BD, EBD, ED, LD, SLD)
- Have students make a chart of the types of loans and their conditions. (ADD, ADHD, LD, SLD)

Chapter 12 Activity Plan: Savings

Objective: To explain savings options and the importance of saving money for the future.

Teaching Activity

1 Have each student identify a purchase he or she would like to make that would require saving money. This purchase could be for goods (such as a car, stereo, or prom dress) or services (such as a trip, college education, or spa retreat). Have each student make a savings plan to save enough money for the purchase. Students should follow the guidelines from the textbook to develop the plan. Students may need to consider readjusting their current spending habits in order to save more money for their purchase.

Accommodations/Modifications

- Have students make a visual time line of their savings plan. (ADD, ADHD, ASD, ELL, FAS, MR, TBI)
- Provide students with a savings account register to record their savings. (ASD, FAS, MR, TBI)
- Have students make a list of ways they could earn extra money for a special purchase. (ADD, ADHD, ASD, BD, EBD, ED, ELL, FAS, LD, MR, OHI, OI, SLD, TBI)
- Have students list people they purchase gifts for and determine how much money they should set aside each month for gift purchases. (ADD, ADHD, LD, SLD)

Teaching Activity

2 Divide the class into small groups. Have each group brainstorm reasons to save money. Groups may want to use the reasons listed in the textbook to categorize their ideas. Have each group make a collage of the reasons students want to or need to save money. Have each group share its ideas with the class.

Accommodations/Modifications

- Visit a bank with students to learn how to open a savings account. (ADD, ADHD, ASD, BD, EBD, ED, ELL, FAS, MR, OI, TBI)
- Have students develop a T-chart to list the benefits of saving money and the drawbacks of not saving money. (ADD, ADHD, BD, EBD, ED, LD, SLD)
- Have students list ways they could save money besides in a bank account. List the benefits and drawbacks of these methods. (ADD, ADHD, LD, SLD)
- Have students make a poster of purchases they would need to save money for. (ASD, ELL, FAS, MR, TBI)

Continued on next page

Teaching Activity

3 Have each student prepare a persuasive speech on the "pay yourself first" principle. Students should develop the presentation for a specific target audience and identify that group's characteristics. Students should practice the presentation with a partner and then deliver it to a group that represents their target audience.

Accommodations/Modifications

- Have students make a list of ways individuals can pay themselves first. (ADD, ADHD, BD, EBD, ED, LD, SLD)
- Have each student determine how much money he or she would like to save each month. Have students calculate how much they would save in one year. (ASD, ELL, FAS, MR, TBI)
- Visit a bank or credit union with students to learn about various types of accounts and how money can be deposited. (ADD, ADHD, BD, EBD, ED, ELL, LD, SLD)
- Have students develop a monthly budget and include a regular contribution to a savings account. (ADD, ADHD, LD, SLD)

Teaching Activity

4 Have students use an online savings calculator like the one at CNN Money at http://cgi.money.cnn.com/tools/savingscalc/savingscalc.html to calculate savings and savings interest over time. Have students determine the amount of time it will take to save a specific amount of money, such as $1,000, $5,000, or $10,000. Following the activity, have students write a short reflection on what they discovered about saving money for their future.

Accommodations/Modifications

- Have students make a poster of purchases they would need to save money for. (ASD, ELL, FAS, MR, TBI)
- Have each student determine how much money he or she would like to save each month. Have students calculate how much they would save in one year. (ASD, ELL, FAS, MR, TBI)
- Have students make a visual time line of their savings plan. (ADD, ADHD, ASD, ELL, FAS, MR, TBI)
- Visit a bank or credit union with students to learn about various types of accounts and how money can be deposited. (ADD, ADHD, BD, EBD, ED, ELL, LD, SLD)

Continued on next page

Teaching Activity

5 Have students work with a partner to investigate one of the basic saving options identified in the textbook (savings accounts, money market accounts, certificates of deposit, or savings bonds). During the research process, students should look for information about safety and risk, liquidity, earnings, taxes, restrictions, and fees and service charges associated with their saving option. After the research has been completed, have the partner groups participate in think-pair-share sessions with other groups to learn about other saving options and to teach others about the saving option they researched.

Accommodations/Modifications

- Have students locate pamphlets or brochures from financial institutions on the various savings options. (ADD, ADHD, BD, EBD, ED, LD, SLD)
- Provide students with a chart to record information about each savings option. (ADD, ADHD, BD, EBD, ED, LD, SLD)
- Visit a bank or credit union with students to learn about various types of accounts and their safety, risk, liquidity, fees, and restrictions. (ADD, ADHD, BD, EBD, ED, ELL, LD, SLD)

Chapter 13 Activity Plan: Investments

Objective: To understand investment terminology and plan for personal investing options.

Teaching Activity

1 Have students use information from The Mint at http://www.themint.org to learn about investing. Students could also use the site's millionaire calculator at http://www.themint.org/tryit/beamillionare.php to estimate when their investments could make them a millionaire. The Mint provides information and activities on many personal financial literacy topics, as well as lesson plans and resources for teachers.

Accommodations/Modifications

- ◆ Have students work with a partner to explore The Mint Web site. (ASD, ELL, FAS, MR, TBI)
- ◆ Provide students with a chart to record investment information from the Web site. (ADD, ADHD, BD, EBD, ED, LD, SLD)
- ◆ Have students develop a time line for becoming a millionaire. (ADD, ADHD, BD, EBD, ED, LD, SLD)
- ◆ Have students locate brochures or pamphlets from banks or other financial institutions about investment options. (ADD, ADHD, BD, EBD, ED, LD, SLD)

Teaching Activity

2 Invite an investment advisor or representative from an investment firm to the classroom to discuss investing and investment options. Prior to the visit, have students prepare questions about the subject. Provide these questions to the speaker in advance. Following the speaker's visit, have each student write a one-page summary of what he or she learned about investing.

Accommodations/Modifications

- ◆ Provide students with a guided notes sheet for the presentation. (ADD, ADHD, BD, EBD, ED, LD, SLD)
- ◆ Have students locate brochures or pamphlets about investment options from banks or other financial institutions. (ADD, ADHD, BD, EBD, ED, LD, SLD)
- ◆ Have students list the benefits and drawbacks of various investments. (LD, SLD)
- ◆ Have students provide an oral summary of what they learned from the speaker. (ASD, ELL, OHI, OI, SLD, TBI, VI)

Continued on next page

Teaching Activity

3 Have students find newspaper or magazine articles about retirement investment options and strategies and information on the Social Security retirement funds in the United States. Have students select two or three of the articles to read and report on to the class. Have the class develop a list of the main points of the articles on the board. Following the reports, have students work in small groups to sort through the main points and develop an outline to better explain the information presented. Have all the groups compile their information to make the most sense of it.

Accommodations/Modifications

- Provide the articles to students. (ADD, ADHD, LD, SLD)
- Enlarge or highlight the most important points in the articles. (ADD, ADHD, ELL, LD, SLD, TBI, VI)
- Have students develop a poster about Social Security retirement funds. (ADD, ADHD, BD, EBD, ED, ELL, SLD, TBI)
- Invite a state representative to the classroom to discuss the Social Security program and benefits. (ADD, ADHD, ASD, BD, EBD, ED, ELL, LD, MR, SLD, TBI)

Teaching Activity

4 Have students participate in a stock market simulation experience, such as StocksQuest Global Stock Game (GSG), available free of charge on MyStocks page at http://library.think-quest.org/3088/, or The Stock Market Game™, available for a fee at http://smgww.org. These programs allow teachers to monitor students' progress throughout the experience. If possible, allow students to use the program for a period of time.

Accommodations/Modifications

- Have students identify specific stocks they would select to invest in. (ADD, ADHD, BD, EBD, ED, SLD, TBI)
- Visit or invite a professional stock market investor to the classroom to share information about his or her work. (ADD, ADHD, BD, EBD, ED, ELL, LD, SLD)
- Have students locate information about stocks in the newspaper. (ASD, ELL, FAS, MR, TBI)
- Have students use the Internet to find stock information. (ADD, ADHD, BD, EBD, ED, LD, SLD)

Continued on next page

Teaching Activity

5 Invite a local attorney to the classroom to discuss estate planning. Have the professional share with students the purpose of wills, how they work, and how they may change throughout a person's life. Also have the person discuss what an executor and a beneficiary are. Have the attorney explain other documents that individuals may need or encounter, such as a living trust, power of attorney, and a living will, and what would happen if a situation occurred in which these documents did not exist. Following the presentation, have students discuss these documents and the personal importance they place on them.

Accommodations/Modifications

- Locate examples of these legal documents for students to view. (ADD, ADHD, BD, EBD, ED, ELL, FAS, LD, MR, SLD, TBI)
- Have students use the Internet to identify why these documents are beneficial. (ADD, ADHD, BD, EBD, ED)
- Provide scenarios and have students determine what type of legal document would best fit each situation. (ADD, ADHD, BD, EBD, ED, LD, SLD)
- Locate newspaper or magazine articles that show examples of these documents being used in court. (ADD, ADHD, BD, EBD, ED, LD, SLD)

Chapter 14 Activity Plan: Insurance

Objective: To describe the types of insurance available and understand the differences between them.

Teaching Activity

1 Have students work in small groups to brainstorm examples of property risks, personal risks, and liability risks that individuals or families may have. Have the groups prioritize the risks in order from highest to lowest and then categorize the risks. Once the risks are categorized, have students identify the types of insurance available for the risks they identified.

Accommodations/Modifications

- Provide examples of risks and have students categorize them. (ASD, ELL, FAS, MR, TBI)
- Have students gather insurance quotes for various insurance coverage types. (ADD, ADHD, BD, EBD, ED, LD, SLD)
- Invite an insurance representative to the classroom to discuss types and costs of insurance coverage and the benefits of having insurance. (ADD, ADHD, BD, EBD, ED, LD, SLD)
- Provide students with various scenarios and have them determine whether the situations involve low or high risk. (ADD, ADHD, BD, EBD, ED, ELL, LD, SLD)

Teaching Activity

2 Have students work with a partner to develop an educational tool to teach others about basic insurance information, such as terms used in the insurance industry, risks and liability, basic insurance principles, types of insurance available, where to find insurance coverage, and application procedures. Have the groups share their materials with other classes, such as consumer math classes, personal finance classes, and other family and consumer sciences classes.

Accommodations/Modifications

- Have students match insurance terms to their definitions. (ELL, FAS, MR, TBI)
- Have students use the Internet to find information about choosing insurance coverage. (ADD, ADHD, LD, SLD)
- Have students use assistive technology or presentation software to develop their educational materials. (ADD, ADHD, BD, EBD, ED, LD, SLD, TBI, VI)
- Invite an insurance representative to the classroom to discuss basic insurance information. (ADD, ADHD, BD, EBD, ED, LD, SLD)

Continued on next page

Teaching Activity

3 Divide the class into four groups. Have each group explore one type of insurance (auto, home, health, or life). Groups should assign each member a specific topic within their insurance type to research. Ask each group to report on the types of coverage available, terms associated with the type of insurance, specific information about liability or coverage, and other details related exclusively to the group's type of insurance. Have each group prepare an electronic slide presentation for the class.

Accommodations/Modifications

- ◆ Provide students with various scenarios and have them determine which type of insurance would be necessary for each situation. (ADD, ADHD, BD, EBD, ED, ELL, LD, SLD)
- ◆ Have students use assistive technology or presentation software for this activity. (ADD, ADHD, BD, EBD, ED, LD, SLD, TBI, VI)
- ◆ Have students describe situations covered and not covered by insurance. (ADD, ADHD, BD, EBD, ED, ELL, LD, SLD, TBI)
- ◆ Provide students with an insurance summary chart to complete during the presentation. (ADD, ADHD, LD, SLD)

Teaching Activity

4 Have students research different types of government health care programs. Students should learn who the recipients of these programs are and how each program works. Students may be able to locate current newspaper or periodical articles related to their topic. Have students share their information with other students who researched different programs and develop a chart to describe each program.

Accommodations/Modifications

- ◆ Invite a representative from a county agency to discuss types of government health care programs available. (ADD, ADHD, BD, EBD, ED, LD, SLD)
- ◆ Provide students with resources for the project. (ADD, ADHD, BD, EBD, ED, LD, SLD)
- ◆ Provide students with a chart to record the information they learn. (ADD, ADHD, LD, SLD)
- ◆ Have students find pamphlets or brochures developed by state and local agencies that describe government health care programs. (ASD, ELL, FAS, MR, OHI, OI, TBI, VI)

Continued on next page

Teaching Activity

5 Invite an insurance representative from a local agency or company to the classroom to discuss the types of insurance with students. Have the professional discuss options for home, life, and auto insurance with the class. Also have the agent discuss rates and coverage of different plans available for the different types of insurance. Following the presentation, have each student write a one-page reflection on the importance of insurance and why individuals and families should have insurance.

Accommodations/Modifications

- ◆ Develop several scenarios describing individuals with and without insurance. Have students predict the outcome of each scenario. (ADD, ADHD, BD, EBD, ED, ELL, LD, SLD, TBI)
- ◆ Have students list the benefits of having insurance. (ASD, ELL, FAS, MR, TBI)
- ◆ Have students obtain online insurance quotes for various types of insurance. (ADD, ADHD)
- ◆ Have students compare and contrast health care costs for both individuals and families. (ADD, ADHD, BD, EBD, ED, FAS, LD, SLD)

Chapter 15 Activity Plan: Persuasion in the Marketplace

Objective: To describe the role of marketing in consumer decision making.

Teaching Activity

1 Have students collect several examples of advertisements for products or services that teens would purchase. Students could locate print advertisements in magazines, flyers, department store mailings, and so on. Students could also print out advertisements from the Internet, record television or radio advertisements, or take photos of billboard or in-store advertisements. Have students identify the methods of persuasion used in each of the ads. Have each student write a critical evaluation of two or three of the advertisements and share it with a partner.

Accommodations/Modifications

- Provide students with, or let them choose, three pictures of celebrities. Have them describe their clothing and explain its impact on teen consumers. (ADD, ADHD, BD, EBD, ED, LD, SLD)
- Have students work with a partner during this activity. (ASD, FAS, MR, TBI)
- Provide students with pictures or advertisements to analyze. (ADD, ADHD, BD, EBD, ED, LD, SLD)
- Have students identify trends and fads in their school. (ADD, ADHD, LD, SLD)

Teaching Activity

2 Have students design their own small business featuring a product they could make or service they could provide. Students can get ideas from the Internet, books, magazines, or stores. Once students have selected a product, they should create a prototype. Then have each student develop a marketing campaign, including a display or poster, a pamphlet or brochure, and a sales presentation. Students should include information about their product, such as target audience, uses, price, and so on. Have each student give the sales presentation to the class and share the marketing materials. If possible, invite local business leaders to the presentations to provide feedback to the students.

Accommodations/Modifications

- Have students use assistive technology for the project. (HI, OHI, OI, TBI, VI)
- As a class, develop a small business to operate within the school. (ADD, ADHD, BD, EBD, ED, ELL, FAS, HI, MR, OHI, OI, TBI, VI)
- Have students work with a partner to develop their business product. (ASD, ELL, FAS, MR, TBI)
- Have students develop marketing materials for an already existing product. (ASD, MR, TBI)

Continued on next page

Teaching Activity

3 After reading the chapter, have each student create a mobile that illustrates the benefits and drawbacks of advertising for consumers. Students should think of the implications of ads for children, teens, adults, the elderly, and families as they evaluate the benefits and drawbacks. Students could use examples of advertisements in their mobile to illustrate the points they want to make. Display the completed mobiles in the classroom.

Accommodations/Modifications

- Have students work with a partner for this activity. (ASD, FAS, MR, TBI)
- Have students list retailers that advertise in various media. (ADD, ADHD, ASD, LD, SLD)
- Have students locate advertisements that connect famous sports stars or celebrities with certain products. (ADD, ADHD, BD, EBD, ED, LD, SLD)
- Have students look for products that promote certain movies or television shows. (ASD, ELL, FAS, MR, TBI)

Teaching Activity

4 Have students brainstorm how stores, businesses, and companies use incentives to encourage consumers to shop at their store or purchase their products. If possible, have students find examples of different incentives. Have students develop a T-chart listing the positives and negatives of incentives. If possible, have the class team with the school store, booster club, or other in-school business to develop and monitor an incentive program.

Accommodations/Modifications

- List the benefits and drawbacks of retail store incentive or rewards programs. (ADD, ADHD, BD, EBD, ED, LD, SLD)
- Discuss why individuals or families may desire to make bulk purchases. (ADD, ADHD, BD, EBD, ED, LD, SLD)
- Have students describe the benefits and drawbacks of having retail store charge cards. (ADD, ADHD, BD, EBD, ED, LD, SLD)
- Have students identify ways manufacturers market to various audiences, such as mothers, children, and teens. (ASD, ELL, FAS, MR, TBI)

Continued on next page

Teaching Activity

5 Have students collect examples of sale promotions in newspapers, sale flyers, or weekly circulars and identify the type of sale. Have students try to find one of each type of sale described in the textbook.

Accommodations/Modifications

- Provide a list of the types of sales students should look for in their search. (ADD, ADHD, BD, EBD, ED, ELL, LD, SLD)
- Visit a store with students to discover how rebates work. (ADD, ADHD, BD, EBD, ED, LD, SLD)
- Have students find coupons for items they would purchase. (ASD, FAS, MR, TBI)
- Enlarge or highlight the fine print in the advertisements so students can see whether any restrictions or exclusions apply to the sales. (ADD, ADHD, BD, LD, SLD, TBI, VI)

Chapter 16 Activity Plan: Shopping Skills

Objective: To identify the characteristics of a confident and responsible consumer.

Teaching Activity

1 Have students investigate the types of retailers in their community. Students should work in small groups to identify at least ten local businesses and categorize them by type. Students may use the categories identified in the textbook or create their own. Groups should write a description of each of the businesses they have listed, including the products offered, a price comparison with other businesses in their list, and the level of quality and expertise of the business.

Accommodations/Modifications

- Provide a chart for students to use for this activity. (ADD, ADHD, BD, EBD, ED, LD, SLD, TBI)
- Have students list and describe stores they have been to and the types of products available at each. (ASD, ELL, FAS, MR, TBI)
- Show students several pictures of products they may purchase throughout their life. Have students tell what type of retailer they would most likely purchase each item from. (ADD, ADHD, ASD, BD, EBD, ED, ELL, FAS, HI, LD, MR, OHI, OI, SLD, TBI)
- Have students study the Yellow Pages of the telephone book to see how businesses are categorized. (ADD, ADHD, BD, EBD, ED, LD, SLD, TBI)

Teaching Activity

2 Have students develop a chart of at least three at-home shopping options. Students should investigate each option and complete the chart with details about the types of products available, cost of items, ease of shopping, convenience, times available for shopping, types of payment, shipping, layaway options, and return procedures. Following the activity, have each student select the at-home shopping option that would best meet his or her needs and the shopping option that would least meet the student's needs. Have students provide reasons for their choices.

Accommodations/Modifications

- Provide guiding questions for students to use in comparing the shopping options. (ADD, ADHD, BD, EBD, ED, LD, SLD)
- Have students visit Web sites to obtain additional information to perform the comparisons. (ASD, ELL, FAS, MR, TBI)
- Have students list the benefits and drawbacks for each shopping option. (ADD, ADHD, BD, EBD, ED, LD, SLD)
- Provide characteristics of each shopping option for students to categorize. (ADD, ADHD, BD, EBD, ED, ELL, FAS, HI, LD, MR, OHI, OI, SLD, TBI, VI)

Continued on next page

Teaching Activity

3 Have students work in small groups to develop a presentation to teach consumers about warranties. Students should describe the purpose of warranties, types, differences and similarities among warranties, and how warranties protect consumers. Students should also describe how consumers can receive assistance if they have a problem with a product or service that is covered by a warranty. Have students describe situations in which a warranty would not be beneficial.

Accommodations/Modifications

- Enlarge and highlight examples of warranty information. (ELL, LD, SLD, TBI, VI)
- Have students visit a retail store to learn about store warranties or service plans offered. (ADD, ADHD, BD, EBD, ED, ELL, LD, SLD)
- Show pictures of items to students and have them determine whether warranties would apply to each. (ASD, ELL, FAS, MR, TBI)
- Have students make a video about warranties for consumers. (ADD, ADHD)

Teaching Activity

4 Arrange for students to taste-test a variety of national, store, and generic brand food products, such as macaroni and cheese dinners, frozen pizzas, milk, and so on. Have students prepare and sample the food without knowing the brand name of the products they are comparing. Have each student sample all varieties of the similar food products and record such information as price, number of servings, and nutritional information, as appropriate. Also have the students record their own description of the products' taste, flavor, ease of preparation, and so on. Have each student determine the food product he or she would select based only on the information available. Once students have made their selections, reveal the brand information for each product they sampled. Engage students in a discussion about their taste preferences and the product brands they selected.

Accommodations/Modifications

- Provide students with a chart to record information during this activity. (ADD, ADHD, BD, EBD, ED, LD, SLD)
- Have students visit a supermarket to locate brand name, store brand, and generic food products. Have them compare prices. (ADD, ADHD, BD, EBD, ED, ELL, LD, MR, SLD)
- Arrange for taste tests in the school to compare and contrast national and store brand products. (ADD, ADHD, BD, EBD, ED, LD, SLD)
- Have students watch a half-hour of children's television programming and record the food products advertised for children. Have them discuss the impacts of this advertising. (ADD, ADHD, ELL, FAS, LD, MR, OHI, OI, SLD, TBI)

Continued on next page

Teaching Activity

5 Provide students with several scenarios that illustrate making a major purchase. Have each student select a scenario and follow steps for comparison shopping. Students should keep a log of the steps taken and the decision-making process they went through to decide what to purchase. Have students share their scenario, the steps involved in their decision, and three reasons to support their final selections.

Accommodations/Modifications

- Provide students with steps for the decision-making process. (ADD, ADHD, BD, EBD, ED, LD, SLD)
- Have students work with a partner for this activity. (ASD, FAS, MR, TBI)
- Have students visit a store to select the item(s) they would purchase. (ADD, ADHD, ASD, BD, EBD, ED, ELL, FAS, HI, LD, MR, OHI, OI, SLD, TBI, VI)
- Have students identify options for buying an item other than purchasing it new. (ADD, ADHD, BD, EBD, ED, LD, SLD)

Chapter 17 Activity Plan: Technology Products

Objective: To determine the best technology products and services to meet individual needs.

Teaching Activity

1 Have students gather information on a variety of wireless phone companies, services, and promotions. Have each student compare and contrast phones, service types, number of minutes included, coverage areas, long-distance options, fees, and features of each plan or company. Students should select the option that would best suit their needs and budget and a wireless phone plan best suited for an adult they know. Have students describe how each plan meets the needs of each individual.

Accommodations/Modifications

- Have students make a collage showing a variety of technology products. (ASD, ELL, FAS, MR, TBI)
- Interview wireless phone users to learn why they purchased their phone and service plan and how they typically use it. (ADD, ADHD, LD, SLD)
- Have students make a video about proper cell-phone etiquette. (ADD, ADHD, BD, EBD, ED)
- Invite the school liaison officer or a police officer to the classroom to discuss the dangers associated with using cell phones while driving. (ADD, ADHD, BD, EBD, ED, LD)

Teaching Activity

2 Have the director of technology for the school district or a technology specialist from a local business visit the classroom to discuss his or her job and the types of technology options and problems the individual manages on a regular basis. Have the speaker discuss the safety and security issues facing companies and schools when they are protecting confidential information. Also, have the technology expert share with students how he or she manages new types of technology and keeps technology systems up-to-date and functioning properly. Following the presentation, have students write a one-page reflection on the positive and negative aspects of a job or career in technology.

Accommodations/Modifications

- Visit a college or university technology lab for students to learn about educational training programs in technology. (ADD, ADHD, BD, EBD, ED, ELL, LD, OHI, OI, SLD)
- Have students find an article that describes how to protect their computer and online activities. (BD, EBD, ED, LD, SLD)
- Provide students with a guided notes sheet for the presentation. (ADD, ADHD, BD, EBD, ED, LD, SLD)
- Visit a computer company with students to find out how it supports the computer and technology needs of businesses and individuals. (ADD, ADHD, BD, EBD, ED, LD, SLD)

Continued on next page

Teaching Activity

3 Have each student select a technology product he or she is interested in purchasing and research it in *Consumer Reports* magazine. Have students prepare a poster about their item, including the features and other factors they need to consider before making a purchase. Then have the students decide which item they would choose to purchase based on their research. Have students present the posters to the class and display them in the classroom.

Accommodations/Modifications

- Provide copies of product reports to students. (ADD, ADHD, BD, EBD, ED, ELL, LD, SLD)
- Visit a technology or an appliance retail store. Have a sales associate describe the differences between products. (ADD, ADHD, ASD, BD, EBD, ED, ELL, FAS, HI, LD, MR, OHI, OI, SLD, TBI, VI)
- Have students work with a partner for this activity. (ASD, ELL, FAS, LD, MR, OHI, SLD, TBI)
- Have students make a poster showing items they are interested in purchasing. (ASD, FAS, MR, OHI, TBI)

Teaching Activity

4 Have students work with a partner to research ways technology is used in education, focusing on methods of delivery (interactive television classrooms, Web-based classes, e-mail, online discussion boards) or technology tools (SMART Boards™, handheld computers, graphing calculators, PDAs, laptop computers, and infant simulators). Have each group give a presentation to the class on the technology and how it is used. Following the presentations, have students write an essay about how they think technology will be used in education in the future.

Accommodations/Modifications

- Invite an occupational therapist to the classroom to discuss the types of assistive technology used in schools. (ADD, ADHD, ASD, BD, EBD, ED, ELL, FAS, HI, LD, MR, OHI, OI, SLD, TBI, VI)
- Have students use a variety of the technological teaching and learning devices available in your school. (ADD, ADHD, BD, EBD, ED, ELL, FAS, HI, LD, MR, OHI, OI, SLD, TBI, VI)
- Have students interview peers who use these technological devices in their classes and find out how they feel about using them. (ADD, ADHD, LD, SLD)
- Have students visit a distance education classroom and, if possible, view a class in progress. (ADD, ADHD, BD, EBD, ED, LD, SLD)

Continued on next page

Teaching Activity

5 Have students work with a partner to develop a newsletter article to guide consumers in choosing phone service, Internet service, a home computer, or another type of technology product or service. Students should use information from the textbook and other sources, such as technology magazines and customer reviews of products or services found on the Internet. Articles should be unbiased and report only factual information. Publish the articles in a newsletter and make it available for teachers and families in the district.

Accommodations/Modifications

- Have students make a video instead of writing articles. (ADD, ADHD, LD, SLD, TBI)
- Arrange a technology education fair at the school or in the community. (ADD, ADHD, BD, EBD, ED, FAS, LD, OHI, OI, SLD, TBI)
- Have students develop a checklist for consumers to use when making technology buying decisions. (BD, EBD, ED, LD, SLD)
- Have students use the telephone book to locate businesses in the community that offer technology services. (ASD, FAS, MR, TBI)

Chapter 18 Activity Plan: Clothing and Grooming

Objective: To describe options for purchasing, selecting, and caring for clothing.

Teaching Activity

1 Have each student develop a collage of photos and pictures that show how clothing meets the physical, intellectual, emotional, and social needs and functions of individuals.

Accommodations/Modifications

- Select pictures to share with the class. Have students identify whether the pictures depict clothing being used for physical, emotional, social, or intellectual functions. (ADD, ADHD, BD, EBD, ED, LD, SLD)
- Provide students with descriptions and visual examples of clothing that meets physical, social, emotional, and intellectual needs. (ASD, ELL, FAS, LD, MR, SLD, TBI)
- Have students work with a partner for this activity. (ASD, FAS, MR, TBI)
- Have students use the Internet to locate pictures of how people use clothing for different functions. (ADD, ADHD, HI, OHI, OI)

Teaching Activity

2 Have each student draw a Venn diagram and select two clothing shopping options to compare and contrast. Students could select from stores, catalogs, Internet, or television shopping options. Have each student research the two options and record the similarities and differences in the diagram.

Accommodations/Modifications

- Provide guiding questions for students to use in comparing and contrasting. (ADD, ADHD, BD, EBD, ED, LD, SLD)
- Have students visit stores to perform the comparisons. (ASD, ELL, FAS, MR, TBI)
- Have students list the benefits and drawbacks of each shopping option. (ADD, ADHD, BD, EBD, ED, LD, SLD)
- Provide a list of characteristics of each shopping option for students to categorize. (ADD, ADHD, BD, EBD, ED, ELL, FAS, HI, LD, MR, OHI, OI, SLD, TBI, VI)

Continued on next page

Teaching Activity

3 Have each student choose an outdoor activity, such as fishing, whitewater rafting, mountain or rock climbing, hiking or backpacking, bicycling, sailing, canoeing, camping, or snowmobiling. Have students plan three complete outfits that would be appropriate for the activity they selected, based on fiber content and characteristics.

Accommodations/Modifications

- Have students plan one or two outfits for this activity rather than three. (ADD, ADHD, BD, EBD, ED, LD, SLD, TBI)
- Have students work with a partner for this activity. (ASD, ELL, FAS, MR, TBI)
- Have students visit a sporting goods store to identify appropriate clothing and accessories for the activity they selected. (ADD, ADHD, BD, EBD, ED, ELL, LD, SLD)
- Provide students with pictures of clothing and accessories and have them identify the activity they are appropriate for. (ASD, FAS, MR, TBI)

Teaching Activity

4 Have each student select five to ten of his or her own garments that require different types of care. Have students record a description of each item and the care information and symbols from the labels. Ask them to bring the information to class for discussion.

Accommodations/Modifications

- Visit a thrift shop with students to look at clothing care requirements on care labels. (ADD, ADHD, BD, EBD, ED, ELL, LD, SLD)
- Photocopy and enlarge clothing care labels. (ASD, ELL, FAS, MR, TBI, VI)
- Have students record the care requirements for three garments rather than five to ten. (ADD, ADHD, LD, SLD)
- Have students draw the symbols used to depict various clothing care directions. (ADD, ADHD, BD, EBD, ED, ELL, FAS, LD, MR, SLD, TBI)

Continued on next page

Teaching Activity

5 Arrange for participants from a local cosmetology training program to visit the classroom. Have the instructor and students share information about grooming and personal hygiene products and services for males and females. If possible, arrange for students in the training program to perform grooming services for students in the class, such as facials, manicures, and haircuts.

Accommodations/Modifications

- Have students make a collage showing products used for personal grooming and hygiene. (ASD, ELL, FAS, MR, TBI)
- Have students make a daily schedule that includes personal grooming and hygiene routines. (ASD, ELL, FAS, MR, TBI)
- Have students make a T-chart showing the benefits of keeping oneself properly groomed and the negatives of poor hygiene. (ADD, ADHD, ASD, BD, EBD, ED, ELL, FAS, MR, OHI, TBI)
- Have students visit the cosmetology training program to learn about career opportunities. (ADD, ADHD, BD, EBD, ED, LD, SLD)

Chapter 19 Activity Plan: Transportation

Objective: To review transportation options and determine personal transportation needs.

Teaching Activity

1 Have students research a mass transit system, such as a bus or subway, in their community, a larger city in their area, or a place they would like to visit. Have students find maps and user information for the system and plan several trips they could take to stores, service agencies, tourist destinations, and other areas of interest. Have students determine the cost of the trips, how to maneuver within the transit system, and other rules, policies, and procedures necessary to use the system.

Accommodations/Modifications

- Take students on an outing and use a mass transit system. (ADD, ADHD, ASD, BD, EBD, ED, ELL, FAS, HI, LD, MR, OHI, OI, SLD, TBI, VI)
- Have students locate transit systems closest to their home, school, or place of employment. (ADD, ADHD, BD, EBD, ED, ELL, LD, SLD)
- Have students make a video demonstrating how to use a mass transit system. (ADD, ADHD)
- Have students make a list of common courtesies to observe when using mass transit systems. (ASD, BD, EBD, ED, MR, TBI)

Teaching Activity

2 Have students use the Internet, magazines, and other media to learn about the benefits of mass transit. Have students use the information they find to develop a public awareness campaign for the general public promoting the use of transit systems.

Accommodations/Modifications

- Have a representative from a mass transit system speak to the class about the benefits of using mass transit services. (ADD, ADHD, BD, EBD, ED, LD, SLD)
- Provide students with resources for the project. (ADD, ADHD, BD, EBD, ED, LD, SLD, TBI)
- Provide a guide describing the process of practical reasoning and questions to ask when researching. (LD, SLD)
- Have students make a poster that encourages others to use mass transit systems. (ADD, ADHD, ASD, ELL, FAS, MR, TBI)

Continued on next page

Teaching Activity

3 Have students locate information on purchasing a vehicle from reputable online sources, such as Utah State University Extension at http://extension.usu.edu/files/fampubs/finan01.pdf. Students should work with a partner to identify the top five things to look for and the top five things to avoid when making a vehicle purchase. Students should compile their lists into a class list and publish it in the school or community newsletter.

Accommodations/Modifications

- Invite a consumer advocate to the classroom to share car-buying tips with students. (ADD, ADHD, BD, EBD, ED, ELL, LD, SLD)
- Have students develop a checklist of things to look for or ask about when buying a vehicle. (ADD, ADHD, LD, SLD)
- Obtain copies of vehicle descriptions from a car dealership for students to read and analyze. (ADD, ADHD, BD, EBD, ED, ELL, LD, SLD, TBI)
- Have students ask several adults for advice on buying a car. (ADD, ADHD, BD, EBD, ED, LD, SLD)

Teaching Activity

4 Have students develop a T-chart to compare and contrast the benefits and drawbacks of buying versus leasing a vehicle. Students should use the Internet and other reliable resources, including automobile sales professionals, to learn the procedures, terms, and policies for each vehicle financing option. After students have developed their chart, have students use the information to write a persuasive essay on the topic.

Accommodations/Modifications

- Invite a car dealership representative to the classroom to discuss the benefits and drawbacks of both buying and leasing a vehicle. (ADD, ADHD, BD, EBD, ED, LD, SLD)
- Obtain copies of vehicle lease policies from a car dealership for students to read and analyze. (ADD, ADHD, BD, EBD, ED, ELL, LD, SLD, TBI)
- Have students determine the difference in monthly payments for purchased and leased vehicles. (ADD, ADHD, BD, EBD, ED, LD, SLD)
- Have students list the responsibilities of car owners. (ADD, ADHD, BD, EBD, ED, ELL, FAS, LD, MR, SLD, TBI)

Continued on next page

Teaching Activity

5 Have each student develop a five-year time line of vehicle ownership. The time line should include all monthly expenses of owning and operating a vehicle, such as payments, insurance, tune-ups, oil changes, tires, batteries, regularly scheduled recommended maintenance, and estimated unexpected maintenance costs. Have students calculate expected yearly and five-year maintance and ownership costs. With these figures, students can determine the daily and monthly costs of owning and maintaining a vehicle.

Accommodations/Modifications

- Visit a car repair shop with students to learn about the services offered and the costs of general car maintenance. (ADD, ADHD, BD, EBD, ED, ELL, LD, SLD)
- Make copies of vehicle owner's manuals to have students use as references for this activity. (ADD, ADHD, ELL, LD, SLD)
- Have students locate advertisements for reduced or sale rates on vehicle maintenance services or products. (ASD, ELL, FAS, MR)
- Invite an auto insurance representative to the classroom to discuss the types and cost of auto insurance coverage. (ADD, ADHD, BD, EBD, ED, LD, SLD)

Chapter 20 Activity Plan: Recreation

Objective: To manage choices about leisure time and recreational activities and expenses.

Teaching Activity

1 Have each student make a collage showing the types of recreational activities he or she participates in for mental, physical, and social health. Have each student locate magazine pictures that represent the activities or bring in photos showing the student participating in activities. Have each student share his or her completed collage with the class. Following the activity, have each student write a short reflection on the benefits of participating in recreational activities that contribute to his or her mental, physical, and social health.

Accommodations/Modifications

- Have students develop a transition portfolio of recreational activities they enjoy. (ASD, ELL, FAS, MR, OHI, OI, TBI)
- Provide students with examples of mental, physical, and social activities. (ADD, ADHD, BD, EBD, ED, ELL, LD, SLD)
- Engage students in a variety of mental, physical, and social recreational activities. (ADD, ADHD, ASD, BD, EBD, ED, ELL, FAS, HI, LD, MR, OHI, OI, SLD, TBI, VI)
- Invite a speaker from the local parks and recreation department to describe recreational opportunities in the community. (ADD, ADHD, ASD, BD, EBD, ED, ELL, FAS, HI, LD, MR, OHI, OI, SLD, TBI, VI)

Teaching Activity

2 Have the class develop a teen's activity guide for their peers. The class should brainstorm ideas for positive recreational activities, hobbies, clubs, etc., in the school and community that high school students could engage in. Have each student research several of the ideas to learn about cost, location, phone number, Web site, times, necessary equipment, and any other pertinent information about each activity. Have students compile their information into one document. Have the class publish the guide, distribute it to other students, and make the guide available in the school office and guidance center.

Accommodations/Modifications

- Develop a form for students to use when locating information on recreational activities. (ADD, ADHD, BD, EBD, ED, ELL, LD, SLD)
- Have students tour several recreation venues to learn about the types of activities they offer. (ADD, ADHD, BD, EBD, ED, ELL, FAS, HI, MR, OHI, OI, TBI, VI)
- Have students develop a video showing recreation activities available in their community. (ADD, ADHD)
- Have students locate recreational facilities and other community locations that are accessible to individuals with disabilities. (ASD, FAS, HI, MR, OHI, OI, TBI, VI)

Continued on next page

Teaching Activity

3 Have each student develop a mobile that represents influences on leisure time. Students should use the factors discussed in the textbook, as well as others they think of, to create a visual depiction of how they consider and select leisure opportunities. Have each student explain his or her mobile to the class. Display the mobiles in the classroom.

Accommodations/Modifications

- Have students identify activities they enjoy doing with family, with friends, and alone. (ASD, ELL, FAS, MR, TBI)
- Have students make a collage showing activities that do not require any money. (ADD, ADHD, BD, EBD, ED, ELL, LD, SLD)
- Have students work with a partner to come up with ideas about influences on their recreational activities. (ASD, FAS, MR, TBI)
- Invite a speaker from the local parks and recreation department to describe recreational opportunities in the community. (ADD, ADHD, ASD, BD, EBD, ED, ELL, FAS, HI, LD, MR, OHI, OI, SLD, TBI, VI)

Teaching Activity

4 Invite a travel agent to the classroom to discuss vacation planning. The agent may also be able to assist students with planning their own vacation scenarios and calculating the cost of travel, lodging, meals, attractions, and so on. Have students prepare questions for the speaker and provide them to the speaker ahead of time.

Accommodations/Modifications

- Have students use travel Web sites to plan a vacation. (ADD, ADHD, BD, EBD, ED, LD, SLD)
- Have a guest speaker share his or her travel experiences. (ADD, ADHD, BD, EBD, ED, LD, MR, SLD, TBI)
- Have students work with a partner to plan a trip or vacation. (ASD, ELL, FAS, MR, TBI)
- Have students bring in vacation pictures or share their own travel experiences. (ASD, BD, EBD, ED, ELL, FAS, HI, MR, OHI, OI, TBI, VI)

Continued on next page

Teaching Activity

5 Have students work in small groups to develop an evaluation tool for assessing parks and other public recreational facilities. The groups could create an original document or gather ideas from documents and Web sites such as the National Recreation and Park Association at www.nrpa.org. If possible, have students use the tool they create to evaluate parks and other public recreational facilities in their community. Students could develop a rating system or a key to use in the evaluation and link their findings to the school's Web site. Students could also publish their evaluation tool and the results of their evaluations in a community newsletter.

Accommodations/Modifications

- Invite a speaker from the local parks and recreation department to describe how workers maintain parks and recreational facilities. (ADD, ADHD, BD, EBD, ED, LD, SLD)
- Have students draw a plan for a park or recreational facility (for example, a skate park or a miniature golf course). (ADD, ADHD, BD, EBD, ED, HI, LD, SLD, TBI)
- Visit community parks with students to perform the evaluations. (ADD, ADHD, BD, EBD, ED, ELL, FAS, HI, LD, MR, OHI, OI, SLD, TBI)
- Organize a group to volunteer time to clean up a local park. (ADD, ADHD, BD, EBD, ED, ELL, FAS, HI, LD, MR, SLD, TBI)
- Have students create maps of community parks or a map showing where parks are located in the community. (ADD, ADHD, LD, SLD)

Chapter 21 Activity Plan: Food and Nutrition

Objective: To make informed decisions about food choices, purchases, and selection.

Teaching Activity

1 Have students create a graphic organizer by folding a sheet of notebook paper in half and then in thirds to create six sections. Have students unfold the paper and label each section with one of the major nutrient classes. In each section, have students identify and record the main function of the nutrient class and examples of foods that supply the nutrient.

Accommodations/Modifications

- ◆ Provide the graphic organizer for students, with the nutrients labeled. (ADD, ADHD, EBD, LD, SLD)
- ◆ Provide students with correct and incorrect examples of nutrient functions for each nutrient and have students highlight the correct examples. (ADD, ADHD, EBD, LD, SLD, TBI)
- ◆ Have students identify foods that supply each of the six nutrients. (ASD, MR, TBI)
- ◆ Have students focus on one of the six nutrients by making a poster that describes the main function of the nutrient and examples of foods that supply the nutrient. (ADD, ADHD, EBD, LD, SLD)

Teaching Activity

2 Have students record all the foods they eat and all the physical activities they engage in for three days. Have students use MyPyramid Tracker at www.mypyramid.gov to analyze their food intake and physical activity. Have students compare their diet and exercise records to what the MyPyramid Plan recommends. Each student should write a personal reflection on his or her analysis from MyPyramid.

Accommodations/Modifications

- ◆ Have the students sort the foods they have recorded into the five food groups. (MR, TBI)
- ◆ Have students use assistive technology for computer applications. (HI, OHI, OI, TBI, VI)
- ◆ Provide students with sample daily food records. (ADD, ADHD, EBD)
- ◆ Have students select magazine pictures to create samples of low-calorie meals and snacks. (ASD, MR, TBI, HI)

Continued on next page

Teaching Activity

3 Have students survey family members to find out their favorite meals. Using the results, have each student develop a month of dinner menus, making sure to include a variety of foods and at least one favorite meal from each person's list each week. Students may need to add side dishes or additional items to make each meal nutritionally balanced. Students should also include a variety of colors, textures, and flavors at each meal. After the month's menu is complete, have students prepare weekly shopping lists for the meals.

Accommodations/Modifications

- Modify the activity by reducing the number of menus required. (ADD, ADHD, BD, EBD, ED, LD, SLD)
- Provide students with supermarket flyers. Have them circle food items for their shopping list. (ASD, FAS, MR, OHI, TBI)
- Have students locate pictures of appealing meals in magazines. (ASD, FAS, MR, TBI)
- Provide a checklist for the types of foods to include in each meal. (ADD, ADHD, BD, EBD, ED, LD, SLD, TBI)

Teaching Activity

4 Gather several copies of menus from various local restaurants. Divide students into small groups and have each group use one of the menus to create a twenty-question scavenger hunt to become more familiar with the menu. Photocopy the groups' questions and distribute them to the other groups to complete the scavenger hunts. Using the same menus, have each student select a meal from the menu that he or she would order. Have the students calculate the cost of the meal and add the appropriate tax to the bill. Students should also determine the correct amount of tip to leave their server.

Accommodations/Modifications

- Enlarge the size of the menu. (MR, OI, VI)
- Highlight menu sections that contain information for this activity. (ADD, ADHD, ELL, FAS, LD, MR, SLD, TBI)
- Have students use a calculator to add up the meal cost, tax, and tip. (ADD, ADHD, BD, EBD, ED, ELL, LD, MR, OHI, SLD, TBI)
- Take students for a dining-out experience. (ADD, ADHD, ASD, BD, EBD, ED, ELL, FAS, HI, LD, MR, OHI, OI, SLD, TBI, VI)

Continued on next page

Teaching Activity

5 Have students use information from food packages and price labels to determine the unit or per-serving cost of a variety of foods. Students should compare the unit or per-serving prices of similar items to ensure that they are getting the most product for their consumer dollar.

Accommodations/Modifications

- ◆ Have students work with a partner for this activity. (ASD, MR, TBI)
- ◆ Have students portion out food to show one reasonable serving. (ADD, ADHD, LD, SLD)
- ◆ Provide a graphic organizer for comparisons. (ADD, ADHD, LD, MR, SLD, TBI)
- ◆ Have students calculate reasonable serving amounts by weight, quantity, and piece. (ASD, MR, TBI)

Chapter 22 Activity Plan: Health Care

Objective: To understand health care services and appraise health care options.

Teaching Activity

1 Have each student use a large piece of construction paper to develop a wellness poster. Have students draw three interlocking circles across the width of the paper and label them physical, emotional, and social. In each circle, have each student list or describe how he or she stays healthy or could become healthy in that area to contribute to his or her overall wellness. Display the posters in the classroom.

Accommodations/Modifications

- ◆ Have students create a poster showing people engaged in healthful activities. (ASD, FAS, MR, OHI, TBI)
- ◆ Have students describe enjoyable things they can do with friends. (ASD, ED, ELL, FAS, MR)
- ◆ Have a health teacher visit the classroom to share wellness strategies. (ADD, ADHD, ASD, BD, EBD, ED, ELL, FAS, HI, LD, MR, OHI, OI, SLD, TBI, VI)
- ◆ Visit a YMCA or other community fitness center with students to learn about the programs and services offered. (ADD, ADHD, ASD, BD, EBD, ED, ELL, FAS, HI, LD, MR, OHI, OI, SLD, TBI, VI)

Teaching Activity

2 Invite the school nurse to the classroom to discuss physical health concerns that adolescents and teens should be aware of, such as asthma, allergies, diabetes, communicable diseases, or obesity. The nurse should review prevention strategies for physical conditions that may impact an individual across the lifespan, such as cancer, heart disease, osteoporosis, and so on. Students should prepare questions for the nurse prior to the visit and provide these questions to the guest in advance. The nurse should also explain what students should do if they would like to discuss their health with a professional.

Accommodations/Modifications

- ◆ Have students practice proper hand washing to reduce the spread of germs. (MR)
- ◆ Have students teach younger children ways to stay healthy and fit. (ADD, ADHD, BD, EBD, ED, LD, SLD, TBI)
- ◆ Have students interview a person with a health condition to learn more about it. (ADD, ADHD, BD, EBD, ED, LD, SLD)
- ◆ View a video that discusses wellness strategies. (ADD, ADHD, ASD, BD, EBD, ED, ELL, FAS, HI, LD, MR, OHI, OI, SLD, TBI, VI)

Continued on next page

Teaching Activity

3 Have students work in small groups to create a guide for consumers, explaining how to use medicines safely. Students should use the textbook information and seek reliable online resources, such as the pamphlet from the U.S. Department of Health and Human Services at http://www.ahrq.gov/CONSUMER/safemeds/safemeds.pdf. Each group might select a different target audience for the information.

Accommodations/Modifications

- Have students read directions and warnings from different types of medicine. (ASD, ELL, FAS, MR, TBI)
- Have students identify ways to keep children safe from accidental poisoning. (ADD, ADHD, BD, EBD, ED, ELL, LD, SLD)
- Have students identify ways pharmacies and drug manufacturers try to prevent misuse of medications. (ADD, ADHD, BD, EBD, ED, LD, SLD)
- Visit a pharmacy with students to learn about prescription drugs and common precautions. (ASD, MR)

Teaching Activity

4 Have a health care administration professional visit the classroom to discuss the mission, goals, and philosophy of his or her organization, along with policies related to patient rights and responsibilities. The representative should describe in detail the types of services the facility offers to patients and the services the facility does not provide. Have the professional discuss how consumers should select quality health care and the importance of maintaining good communication with health care providers. Following the presentation, have students describe what they would look for when selecting health care providers for themselves and their family and also the types of questions they would ask a health care professional during an initial visit.

Accommodations/Modifications

- Tour a hospital or clinic with students. (ADD, ADHD, ASD, BD, EBD, ED, ELL, FAS, HI, LD, MR, OHI, OI, SLD, TBI, VI)
- Have students make a list of the characteristics they would look for in a doctor or other health care provider. (ASD, ELL, FAS, MR, TBI)
- Locate places in the community where families can receive free or reduced-cost health care services. (ADD, ADHD, BD, EBD, ED, ELL, FAS, HI, LD, MR, OHI, OI, SLD, TBI, VI)
- Have students make a list of their health care providers, their phone numbers, and addresses. (ASD, ED, ELL, FAS, MR, TBI)

Continued on next page

Teaching Activity

5 Have students research aspects of quality care in child or adult care services and facilities. Students could use the textbook, other print resources, reputable online resources, and interviews with parents or adults who provide care for elderly adults. Have students compile the information they've gathered into a pamphlet to educate consumers who may be seeking these services. Make these educational resources available at the public library, city hall, county courthouse, and other public buildings.

Accommodations/Modifications

- Tour a quality child care facility with students. (ADD, ADHD, ASD, BD, EBD, ED, ELL, FAS, HI, LD, MR, OHI, OI, SLD, TBI, VI)
- Tour a quality adult care facility with students. (ADD, ADHD, ASD, BD, EBD, ED, ELL, FAS, HI, LD, MR, OHI, OI, SLD, TBI, VI)
- Have students work with a partner for this activity. (ASD, ELL, FAS, MR, TBI)
- View a video on selecting quality child or adult care services. (ADD, ADHD, BD, EBD, ED, ELL, FAS, LD, MR)

Chapter 23 Activity Plan: Housing and Furnishings

Objective: To identify housing options and describe procedures for furnishing and maintaining a home.

Teaching Activity

1 Have the class consider a typical family's needs, wants, and priorities for housing across the lifespan. Have students work in small groups to develop a scenario of a fictional family at a particular stage of the family life cycle. Have each group exchange scenarios with another group. Have the students find examples of housing that would meet the needs, wants, and priorities of the family described in the scenario. Have students share the scenarios and their recommendations with the rest of the class.

Accommodations/Modifications

- Have students sketch a floor plan for the scenarios. (ADD, ADHD, BD, EBD, ED, LD, SLD)
- Tour various forms of housing with students. (ADD, ADHD, BD, EBD, ED, ELL, LD, MR, OHI, OI, SLD, TBI)
- View a closed-captioned video about housing options. (ADD, ADHD, ASD, BD, EBD, ED, ELL, FAS, HI, LD, MR, OHI, OI, SLD, TBI)
- Have students think about their own home and how it meets (or does not meet) their family's needs. (ADD, ADHD, HI, SLD)

Teaching Activity

2 Have each student develop a three-dimensional model to represent the advantages and disadvantages of both buying and renting. Students should use the textbook, online resources, and interviews with homeowners and renters to learn the pros and cons of each housing option. Students should include a minimum of five advantages and five disadvantages of each option in their model. Have students share their completed model with the class. Display the models in the school's library or other area for public viewing.

Accommodations/Modifications

- Have students make a chart of the advantages and disadvantages of buying and renting. (ADD, ADHD, BD, EBD, ED, ELL, LD, SLD, TBI)
- View a closed-captioned video on buying a home or renting an apartment. (ADD, ADHD, ASD, BD, EBD, ED, ELL, FAS, HI, LD, MR, OHI, OI, SLD, TBI, VI)
- Have students work with a partner on this activity. (ASD, ELL, MR, SLD, TBI)
- Provide students with ideas for the models. (ADD, ADHD, ELL, FAS, LD, SLD, TBI)

Continued on next page

Teaching Activity

3 Invite a real estate agent or home buying expert to the class to discuss family housing selection and purchases. Have the speaker discuss the financial and personal obligations of home ownership. The speaker could also talk about the process of buying a home and the benefits of home ownership.

Accommodations/Modifications

- Have students tour a home that is for sale or an apartment that is for rent. (ADD, ADHD, BD, EBD, ED, ELL, FAS, HI, LD, MR, OHI, OI, SLD, TBI)
- Have students take notes during the presentation. (ADD, ADHD, BD, EBD, ED, LD, SLD)
- Provide students with points to listen for during the presentation. (ADD, ADHD)
- Have students locate homes for sale in the newspaper. (ADD, ADHD, BD, EBD, ED, ELL, LD, SLD)

Teaching Activity

4 Have each student develop a chart of the daily, weekly, monthly, and annual home cleaning and maintenance tasks that must be performed in their home. Have the students take the lists home to discuss with their family and add any additional tasks. Next to each task, have students identify the family member(s) responsible for performing the task or ensuring that the task is completed.

Accommodations/Modifications

- Provide a list of tasks and have students record who performs them. (ASD, MR, TBI)
- Provide a chart template for students to complete. (ADD, ADHD, BD, EBD, ED, LD, SLD)
- Have students make a list of their own daily or weekly chores. (ADD, ADHD, ASD, BD, EBD, ED, ELL, FAS, MR, OHI, OI, TBI, VI)
- Have students list the name of each person in their family and describe each person's chores. (ASD, FAS, MR, TBI)

Continued on next page

Teaching Activity

5 Locate several copies of apartment leases. Have students compare and contrast the components and requirements of each lease. Students should look up and define unfamiliar terms. If possible, arrange for the class to tour an apartment complex and learn about the process for and responsibilities of renting an apartment.

Accommodations/Modifications

- Have students practice completing sample leases or renting applications. (ADD, ADHD, BD, EBD, ED, ELL, LD, SLD)
- Enlarge the forms for students. (ASD, MR, OHI, OI, VI)
- Have students calculate the rent payments for one year. (ADD, ADHD, LD, SLD)
- Have students list the rules for living in an apartment. (ADD, ADHD, BD, EBD, ED, ELL, LD, MR, OHI, SLD, TBI)